GREAT CONS & CON ARTISTS

GREAT CONS & CON ARTISTS

THE INCREDIBLE STORIES
OF THE MASTERS OF DECEIT

ROBIN
LANGLEY
SOMMER

COURAGE
B O O K S
AN IMPRINT OF
RUNNING PRESS BOOK PUBLISHERS

9 8 7 6 5 4 3 2 1

Digit on the right indicates the number of
this printing.

Library of Congress Cataloging-in-
Publication Number 93-87599

ISBN 1-56138-454-2

Printed and bound in China.

Cover designed by Toby Schmidt.

First published by Courage Books,
an imprint of
Running Press Book Publishers
125 South Twenty-second Street
Philadelphia, Pennsylvania 19103-4399

Front cover, clockwise from top: Cassie
Chadwick (UPI/Bettmann), Ivar Kreuger
(The Bettmann Archive), Pierre Teilhard de
Chardin (at right) (UPI/Bettmann), Charles
Ponzi (UPI/Bettmann), John W. Keeley (The
Bettmann Archive), an advert for a quack
medicine (The Bettmann Archive),
Ferdinand Waldo Demara (UPI/Bettmann),
and Phineas T. Barnum (The Bettmann
Archive).

Back cover: Stub Newall's "Cardiff Giant"
(The Bettmann Archive).

PAGE 1: Herschel's
telescope supposedly
allowed the observer a
close-up view of the
Moon.

PAGES 2-3: During the
nineteenth century, a
plethora of pseudo-
medical remedies,
claiming universal and
miraculous powers of
healing, and promising
a complete cure, were
targeted at gullible
customers.

RIGHT: The "Piltdown
Man" was one of the
most notorious hoaxes
of the twentieth
century. This
photograph of the
Piltdown site, taken
around 1913, shows
excavations in
progress.

CONTENTS

STILL SEARCHING AT PILTDOWN

A ROGUES' GALLERY OF CON ARTISTS

Most of us have a perverse fascination with the great con artists of this world, whether hoaxers, swindlers, forgers, imposters, pitchmen, or outright crooks. Their effrontery and ingenuity in fleecing their fellow citizens through the ages may be deplorable, but it often has a humorous side – especially if someone else is the victim. Classic "cons" may become part of a nation's folklore, like the selling and reselling of the Brooklyn Bridge to credulous tourists. In France, the notorious confidence man "Count" Victor Lustig is remembered as the man who sold the Eiffel Tower. Then there was Sweden's Ivar Kreuger, who built a financial empire in the depths of a worldwide depression and became known as

"the greatest swindler the world has ever known."

Kreuger, nicknamed the "Match King," grew rich during World War I when he acquired a monopoly of Sweden's potash and phosphorus supplies and seized control of the nation's match-making industry. He rapidly parlayed the holding company he called Swedish Match into a stock-and-bond operation with almost limitless credit that made billions of dollars worth of paper "state loans" to European governments during the heady, free-spending 1920s.

Kreuger's fortune, like that of most con men, was built on an uncanny ability to lie persuasively and to manipulate the public and the media. In his book *Great Swindlers*,

PAGE 6: P. T. Barnum, whose circus was proclaimed as "The Greatest Show on Earth."

LEFT: "Count" Victor Lustig leaves the Federal Court in handcuffs in 1935, having been sentenced to 20 years in jail.

BELOW: Swedish "Match King" Ivar Kreuger (right).

Professor A. F. L. Deeson quotes an American journalist of the day on his impressions of Kreuger's 125-room headquarters in Stockholm: "The moment you pass the finely wrought gates you get the atmosphere of some continental palace. Instead of the dusty, tarnished splendor of a departed day, however, it is bright gleaming. Massive marble columns surround what the French call a court of honor. In the center is a bronze fountain surmounted by a graceful, poised figure of Diana."

Kreuger kept a battery of telephones on his desk, including one that was a dummy used to impress visitors. He could ring it by pressing a button under his desk, then pretend he was talking with one of the crowned heads of Europe or a world-famous financier. It was also useful in escaping unwanted visitors; he could announce that he had been summoned away on urgent business. When he traveled to the United States

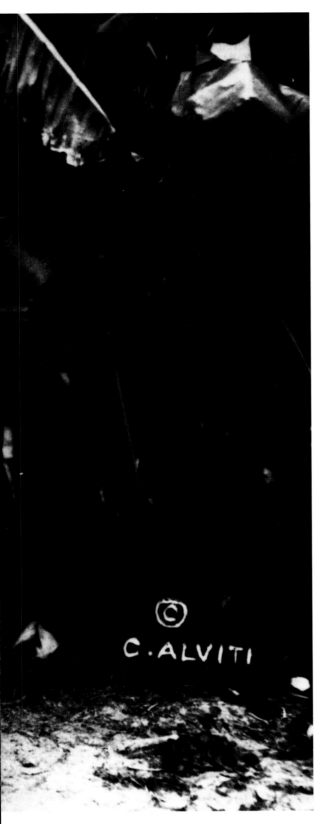

C. ALVITI

on the *Berengaria*, he arranged to tie up the ship's wireless room for 24 hours so that fellow passengers and reporters meeting the ship would know how important he was. "Extreme pressure of business," he replied coolly to all inquirers. Everyone was impressed, including Percy A. Rockefeller, who became a director of International Match.

The bill finally came due in 1932, after Kreuger had extended his holdings to in-

clude mines, railroads, timber interests, film companies, and real estate. As Deeson describes it: "No sooner had he acquired a tangible asset than he would start borrowing on it – not legally once, but illegally many times over. On the basis of millions in actual profits from the Match companies, and by manipulations of the books of Kreuger and Toll and the subsidiary companies, he was in fact creating hundreds of millions in dubious profits."

The stock market crash of 1929 made it inevitable that this shaky edifice would collapse, as Kreuger took enormous losses on the New York Stock Exchange in an effort to stave off disaster. The upswing he counted on after the crash never came, and when he took his own life in a Paris hotel room, the claims on his estate totaled $585 million.

Another swindler of breathtaking proportions was Italian-born Charles Ponzi, known as "the man who invented money." He began as a petty thief in his home town, graduated to robbing poor boxes at the local church, and sailed for America in steerage in 1901, cardsharping his way across the Atlantic. Unfortunately, there were far more experienced hands at crooked gambling aboard, and he landed at Ellis Island with only $2.50 of his original $250 bankroll.

After a short stint as a dishwasher and waiter, he made his way to Canada, where he was arrested for forgery in Montreal. In 1908 he was jailed in Atlanta, Georgia, for smuggling aliens into the United States. Ten years later, the resilient Ponzi surfaced again in Boston. He got work as a messenger at the import-export firm of J. P. Poole and was soon promoted to clerk. In that position, he discovered that postal exchange coupons purchased abroad could be sold for 10 times more in the United States. (The redemption rate was fixed by treaty and had no relation to the exchange rate; thus a postal reply coupon bought in Spain for an American penny could be redeemed in the United States for 10 cents.)

Soon afterward, Ponzi opened an office in Boston and advertised for would-be investors, promising to double their money within 90 days. He made good on the promise by paying out to early investors the money received from later investors. So great was the demand that he opened a New York office a few months later and began taking in $200,000 a day. He reduced the pay-out period to 45 days and became a millionaire in short order. It was a replay of William Miller's classic Peter-to-Paul swindle of 1899: Ponzi never invested a penny of his clients' money in postal reply coupons. He just kept taking it in, returning dollar for dollar on invested monies – until the *Boston Globe* exposed the whole scheme, creating

LEFT: Charles Ponzi, "the man who invented money." Born in Italy, Ponzi's colorful career grew from petty thieving to cardsharping and forgery. Ten years after serving a prison sentence, the resilient Ponzi had become a millionaire, by means of a con based on the humble postal reply coupon.

a run on his company. After paying out $15 million of the $20 million he had acquired over a year, Ponzi was arrested and sent to Plymouth Prison for four years. To no one's surprise, he got out on appeal in 1925 and headed for Florida, where he was soon re-arrested for a real-estate confidence game.

While simple greed is the main motive behind many deceptions, others are fueled by lust, power, recognition, revenge, fame, fantasy, and just plain fun. Sometimes a con that begins as a joke escalates out of control, as in the case of the Great Wall of China hoax of 1899. It began with four bored and tired reporters having coffee in Denver's Hotel Oxford while racking their brains for a story to turn in for the morning edition. In the absence of any exciting news, they decided to collaborate on submitting four different reports that a team of American demolition experts was planning to blow up part of the Great Wall of China and then re-build it.

This wildly improbable story not only made Denver front pages for several days, it was picked up by other papers across the country. Two weeks later, it made headlines on the East Coast, complete with charts, graphs, and confirmation of the report by a Chinese visitor to New York. In June 1900 the news reached China. There a seething

state of unrest about Western encroach-ments on Chinese sovereignty had pro-duced a secret society dedicated to denouncing Western businessmen in China. The members called themselves the Order of Literary Patriotic Harmonious Fists. When they learned that Americans were plotting to destroy the historic Great Wall, a violent uprising broke out in which thou-sands were killed, Chinese and Westerners alike. It is interesting to wonder whether this uprising, called the Boxer Rebellion, would ever have occurred had four Denver reporters not faced a slow news day.

As Kurt Andersen pointed out in an essay for *Time* magazine (September 20, 1993): "Hucksterism is a deeply American trait. P. T. Barnum was a truer man of his time and place than Henry James, and sharpies' nineteenth-century land-promoting broad-sides sucked more settlers west than any high-minded exhortations to manifest destiny. If England is a nation of shop-keepers, the U. S. is a land of pitchmen; it is part of the national charm."

Phineas T. Barnum's career is a case study in successful conning. Born in Bethel, Connecticut, in 1810, he migrated to New York City during his twenties and made his first pitch at Niblo's Garden, where he ex-hibited Joice Heth, a black woman alleged

BELOW: American infantrymen in Peking move forward during the Boxer Rebellion in 1900. It is interesting to speculate whether the uprising of the Order of Literary Patriotic Harmonious Fists would have happened had four bored American journalists not concocted their inflammatory but imaginative story.

LEFT: P. T. Barnum's original American Museum in New York City exhibited "freaks of nature" to avid visitors. The museum later burned down.

to be 161 years old and the nursemaid of George Washington. Crowds flocked to see her, proving Barnum's famous adage that "There's a sucker born every minute."

When interest died down, the budding showman took an ad in the paper to announce that Joice Heth was a robot, not a real person: "What purports to be a remarkably old woman is simply a curiously constructed automaton, made up of whalebone, india-rubber, and numberless springs ingeniously put together and made to move at the slightest touch." The crowds flocked back.

By 1842 Barnum had made enough money to open Scudder's American Museum in New York City. There he exhibited all kinds of curiosities and alleged freaks of nature, making a fortune before the museum burned down. He reopened with the midget he called Tom Thumb – Charles S. Stratton, a perfectly proportioned child whom he had discovered at the age of five and who never grew more than 25 inches tall. In 1844 he took Tom Thumb to England, where the two were presented to Queen Victoria. Barnum's reputation grew even greater when he introduced the stage performer Jenny Lind, "the Swedish Nightingale," to American audiences in 1850.

In 1871 Barnum organized his famous circus – "The Greatest Show on Earth." The

LEFT: Tom Thumb, alias Charles Sherwood Stratton, is dwarfed by his patron P. T. Barnum. Born in Connecticut in 1838, "General Tom Thumb" died in 1883.

FAR RIGHT: Burt Lancaster as the flawed revivalist preacher Elmer Gantry.

RIGHT: Barnum's New American Museum at 539-541 Broadway replaced the earlier version which had succumbed to fire. The New American Museum featured Tom Thumb and equaled its predecessor in popularity.

BELOW: ''Jumbo'' the African elephant was bought by Barnum from the London Zoo in 1882. This ''towering monarch'' and ''prodigious pet'' soon added his name to our vocabulary as ''the universal synonym for all stupendous things.''

company traveled in its own railroad cars rather than the original circus wagons, and its colorful sideshows, parades, acrobats, and menagerie became legendary. Barnum added new words to the language, like ''ballyhoo'' and ''jumbo.'' The original Jumbo was a giant African elephant that he bought from the London Zoo in 1882. Then there was the original ''white elephant'' – *Toung Taloung* – which had to be repainted every time it rained.

America's enduring fascination with the con artist is seen in such movies as *Elmer Gantry* (1960), in which Burt Lancaster gave an award-winning performance as a revivalist preacher who sold out the Gospel for money and power. Michael Caine was memorable as *Alfie*, whose betrayals in love brought him to places he had never wanted to go. (The picture also spawned a popular song that asked rhetorically, ''What's it all about Alfie? Is it just for the moment we live?'') In the 1973 film *The Sting*, early American con man Charley Gondorf was transformed into the modern-day Henry, who took the confidence game to new heights.

ABOVE: ''The Swedish Nightingale,'' coloratura Jenny Lind, pictured in 1850.

RIGHT: A still from the ever-popular film *The Sting*.

ABOVE: Comedian Jack Benny obviously enjoying counting his money. Unfortunately for him, Benny would lose an alleged $300,000 in the Home-Stake Production Company fraud.

RIGHT: Bob Dylan was supposedly another eminent victim of Robert S. Trippet's oil-well scam, but he was in good company: fellow casualties allegedly included Liza Minnelli and Barbra Streisand.

Conversely, many film stars or their accountants have been taken in by schemes like Robert S. Trippet's Home-Stake Production Company, which purported to provide tax shelters for the wealthy by digging nonexistent oil wells. Trippet faced $100,000,000 worth of fraud charges in 1974, after allegedly fleecing such celebrities as talent agent Martin Bergman, Liza Minnelli, Barbra Streisand, Bob Dylan, and Barbara Walters. In his book *Hustlers and Con Men*, Jay Robert Nash tells the amusing story of how tight-wad comedian Jack Benny got the bad news in a phone call from *Chicago Sun-Times* columnist Irv Kupcinet:

"Ever hear of the Home-Stake Production Company?" Kup asks him.

"Never," Benny responds.

"Then I've got some good news and some bad news for you."

Says Benny: "Give me the good news first."

"Your picture is on practically every page one in the country."

"Hey, that's great. What's the bad news?"

"You lost $300,000."

Comes the wail: "Whaaaaat?"

It all goes to show that pitchmen succeed because people want to be fooled. The lure of money and celebrity, however specious, is preferred to reality. As Kurt Andersen concludes in his essay for *Time*: "When television's cutting edge, MTV, consists of record ads passing as entertainment, where millions of people hoot and holler at pro 'wrestling' matches they know to be utterly fake, of course women want to wear a pair of Joan Rivers' QVC earrings, splash on Elizabeth Taylor's White Diamonds, and curl up with a copy of Ivana Trump's *Free to Love*. They aren't bothered by the artifice; they buy the lie."

CHAPTER ONE

HOAXES OF HISTORIC PROPORTIONS

PAGE 18: One of an army of British inflatable vehicles used to mislead German Intelligence in the runup to D-Day in World War II.

RIGHT: Scotsman John Law, whose actions bankrupted France in 1720.

It takes a larger-than-life confidence man to bring financial ruin upon an entire country. That's what Scotsman John Law did to France in 1720. His father, a banker, taught him finance, and Law became a director of the Bank of Amsterdam. This connection led to a friendship with the Duke of Orleans, who would become regent for France's Louis XV. In due time, Law was appointed head of the Banque Général and then Controller-Général of French finances.

The extravagance and ambition of Louis XIV had cost the country $625 million worth of debts. Law's plan for resolving the crisis involved floating paper currency, debasing the coinage, and exciting speculation in the stock of an imaginary "Mississippi Company," which was described as a scheme to develop the rich resources of French Louisiana. With the approval of the duke and the French government, Law opened elegant offices in the Hôtel de Soissons in 1717.

From the outset, there was feverish trading in the stock. Poor people bought and resold it at 120 percent profit to others desperate to cash in on the scheme. They retired on the proceeds, while thousands of others flocked to Paris to buy the stock as word reached the provinces. Housing in the city was so scarce that people paid $4000 per month to rent places that had gone for a pittance the year before. It was reported that a cobbler had rented out his stall to brokers by the day and become a wealthy man. By the

summer of 1720, a 500-livre share of Mississippi Company stock was worth an astonishing 18,000 livres.

Not a single trading ship of the nonexistent company left French ports for the North American interior, but thousands of shares had changed hands in a classic "Peter-to-Paul" swindle. That summer, the Mississippi Bubble burst. The stock was exposed as a fraud. A lynch mob stormed Law's offices, but he had prudently fled across the border disguised as a beggar – which indeed he was, having left behind a fortune in gold and jewels. Even so, he was more for-

LEFT: John Law promised the citizens of France that his "Mississippi Company" would reap the vast wealth contained in the New World's French Louisiana – an enormous tract of land.

BELOW: A scathing contemporary French satire relating the sorry tale of the "Mississippi Bubble" in biting detail.

ABOVE: This engraving, annotated both in French and Dutch, is dedicated to posterity ''in memory of the incredible folly of 1720'' and depicts the hysteria generated by the Mississippi and South Sea Bubbles, and also the human misery that was to result.

RIGHT: An English lampoon, entitled ''The Bubblers Medley,'' pours ridicule on the respective ''Bubbles'' of Holland, England and France. Note the playing card depicting a knave, and the figure blowing bubbles in the lower right-hand corner.

tunate than his predecessor Richard Town, who had been hanged by his irate creditors for a similar scheme in London eight years before.

While Law was reducing France to penury, Robert Harley, later Earl of Oxford and Mortimer, used his influence to wreak havoc on English finances. Soon after he was appointed Chancellor of the Exchequer in 1710, he formed the South Sea Company, which seized the imagination of British financiers. The company assumed a national debt of some 10 million pounds in return for a monopoly of British trade with South America and the South Sea (South Pacific) islands. For several years, the company prospered, but its prospects were highly overrated by speculators. In 1719 it was announced that government creditors could exchange their claims for stock, which created a rush to buy into the seemingly sound company.

Within six months, South Sea Company stock rose from 128½ to 1000. The frenzy of public speculation created a climate in which imitators and swindlers thrived, to the detriment of honest enterprises and investors. In August 1720, at the same time that the Mississippi scheme was exposed, the South Sea Bubble collapsed with the alarming news that fraud had been discovered in the company's management. The stock plummeted and thousands were ruined. However, the company was reorganized after Harley's disgrace and resumed business in headquarters on Threadneedle Street, where it operated until 1852.

Across the Atlantic, colonial confidence men were taking in their fellow citizens in the best entrepreneurial style. Peddlers hawked their sometimes dubious wares throughout the original 13 Colonies. Gamblers and cardsharps plied the Mississippi on paddle-wheelers before the Civil War. Pretenders to a place in High Society bilked the *nouveau riche* of New York and Philadelphia, while anonymous drifters fleeced the public with games of three-card monte and banco (from which the word ''bunk'' was derived). During the late 1860s, hustlers like ''Hungry Joe'' Lewis made up to $100,000 a year preying on wealthy suckers who were too embarrassed to prosecute them. Lewis once took visiting British poet Oscar Wilde for $1500 in an all-night card game fueled by copious amounts of liquor.

Women, too, were making confidence games a way of life. New Yorker Sophie Lyons, who married the notorious bank robber Ned Lyons, was one of them. Pinkerton detectives estimated that she made more than a million dollars during the late nineteenth century. The New York underworld was aghast when she went to work for the *New York World* – as the nation's first gossip columnist.

Cassie Chadwick, the daughter of a poor Toronto family, came to New York in her teens and passed herself off as the illegitimate daughter of steel tycoon Andrew

Carnegie. She spread the story that Carnegie had given her $12 million worth of stock certificates to save and invest. N.Y. investment-bank brokers jumped at the chance to lend her money on the strength of her alleged collateral – an envelope stuffed with newspaper clippings that was locked up in a safety deposit vault for years.

Chadwick went from one bank to another, borrowing money to finance a luxurious style of living all over the country. Her deception was revealed only with the stock-market crash at the turn of the century, when banks up and down the East Coast called in her loans. Her career, and her life, ended in prison.

Another durable female imposter of the day was Ellen Peck (born Nellie Crosby), who took to a life of crime in her early fifties after quietly raising a family with her hus-

band Richard in Sparkville, New York. Moved by an obscure impulse to add excitement to her golden years, she took off for New York City in the spring of 1880 and made a conquest of one B. T. Babbit, an aging millionaire who had made his fortune in soap. On a visit to his office, she slipped $10,000 in negotiable bonds under her dress, then charged him $10,000 to act as a private investigator into the theft, which she assured him was an inside job.

Robber baron Jay Gould was taken for a small fortune by the same late-blooming con woman. So were diamond merchant John D. Grady, Brooklyn physician Christopher Lott, and dozens of others. Peck was accosted by police at her Sparkville home at the age of 84, after she had conned a Latin American businessman out of several plantations on a steamer to Vera Cruz. She told the police indignantly that she was "a devoted wife and a hard-working mother."

She died shortly thereafter, genuinely mourned by the husband who had stood by her through years of desertion, notoriety, and prison terms. He eulogized her as "a victim of circumstances and her own generosity." Poor Richard Peck was perhaps her most gullible conquest.

RIGHT: A plan of the City of New York in November 1803. In 1824 a retired carpenter by the name of Lozier had little difficulty in persuading the city fathers to agree to the most incredible proposal in order to avert the apparently imminent danger of Manhattan Island sinking into the sea. The island would be sawn off, reversed and then reattached to the mainland.

Nineteenth-century New York was the scene of a brilliant hoax perpetrated by a retired carpenter named Lozier with a grandiose sense of humor. He appeared at the mayor's office one day in 1824 to warn him that the entire island of Manhattan was sinking into the sea because of the weight of the tall buildings downtown. To prove it, he pointed out that all the streets ran downhill from City Hall to the Battery.

Lozier suggested that every unemployed carpenter in town should be hired to saw off Manhattan Island at the northern end, row it into New York Harbor, turn it around, then row it back and reattach it to the mainland by the stronger end. Incredibly, the city fathers swallowed this whole and put Lozier in charge of the project. Soon the docks rang to the sound of hammers and lathes, as workmen put up hasty barracks to house the 300 men hired to saw and row.

Livestock was sent downtown to feed the workers as needed, and the waterfront was a bedlam of bawling cattle and clucking chickens. Hogs rooted in their pens and added their grunts to the din. At last, the big

LEFT: Artur Alves Reis, a Portuguese embezzler, whose greatest scam was to persuade the London printing company Waterlow & Sons, Ltd. to print $5,000,000 in 500- and 1000-escudo notes – supposedly "for use in the Portuguese colony of Angola," but actually for his own personal use.

day arrived, and most of the city turned out to watch the sawing off of New York's lower end. Hours went by as the crowd grew angrier and more restless. Then someone discovered a note from Lozier: he had been forced to leave town unexpectedly on account of his health. The irate mob formed a posse to catch the hoaxer, but he got away without a trace, and the sinking of Manhattan became a minor footnote in Gotham history.

The phrase "a license to print money" might have been invented by the Portu-

guese swindler Artur Alves Reis, who carried out one of the boldest financial deceptions of the twentieth century. While serving prison sentence for embezzlement, Alves Reis conceived the idea of having the British firm that printed money for the national bank of Portugal print 100 million escudos for his own account. With the help of three shady confederates, and forged credentials as an operative of the Bank of Portugal, he appeared at the venerable printing firm of Waterlow & Sons, Ltd., London, late in 1924.

There he persuaded the company to print some $5,000,000 worth of 500- and 1,000-escudo notes ''for use in the Portuguese colony of Angola,'' where he had gone to seek his fortune in 1916. He contrived a rationale for reusing serial numbers from a previous printing to bypass the major hurdle faced by all counterfeiters and forgers – use of unauthorized serial numbers. Waterlow & Sons believed his tale that the notes would be surprinted with the words ''For circulation in Angola only'' before the High Commissioner delivered them to the West African colony.

In February 1925 Alves Reis and his coconspirators took delivery on the first suitcase full of brand-new notes and put them into circulation through their own newly founded bank in Oporto, then a center for black-market currency exchanges. They also opened bank accounts in Lisbon, deposited the notes, and started making withdrawals within the week. Soon their conspicuous spending was exciting suspicion.

Alves Reis bought a four-story mansion and spent $25,000 on jewelry for his wife. He strolled through Lisbon in a banker's double-breasted gray suit, sporting a gray homburg and a malacca cane, the picture of self-satisfied elegance. But the rumors spread, and unease was rampant among Portuguese financiers. It was said that shopkeepers in southern Portugal were unwilling to accept the new notes, which bore the likeness of Portuguese navigator Vasco da Gama. Newspapers took up the story, and the Bank of Portugal had to publish a statement in support of the notes to allay public anxiety. Finally, late in 1925, an Oporto branch of the national bank discovered four pairs of Vasco da Gama notes bearing identical serial numbers.

When the Oporto police raided the conspirators' Banco de Angola e Metropole, they found Alves Reis and his confederates in the cellars with suitcases full of escudo notes from the last printing of 200,000. To that date, almost $3 million worth of forged bank notes had been exchanged, and panic ensued when the government announced that the 1924 issue of Vasco da Gama notes was being recalled.

Fortunately, Waterlow had imprinted the second lot of spurious notes with a secret mark, so of the seven million 500-escudo notes presented for exchange, half a million were genuine and the rest were withdrawn from circulation. Alves Reis and his confederates were tried in Lisbon in May 1926 and received long terms of imprisonment for fraud and currency offenses, followed by exile. Today, Lisbon has few memories of the Alves Reis affair, apart from the mansion known locally as the ''Golden Boy Palace.''

England's best-known hoaxer is Horace de Vere Cole, whose exploits are described by Norman Moss in his book *The Pleasures of Deception.* Cole began his career as ''the prince of practical jokers'' at the turn of the century. At Trinity College, Cambridge, he and Adrian Stephen, brother of the future novelist Virginia Woolf, got three friends involved in a scheme to stage a visit to Cambridge by the Sultan of Zanzibar and his entourage, then in England. They went to a theatrical costumers in London for costumes and make-up, then wired the mayor of Cambridge in the name of the Colonial Office to announce that the sultan would be visiting and should be treated royally.

In full regalia, they descended on the college town to be entertained at the Guildhall, taken on a guided tour by hansom cab, and feted at a charity bazaar, where the wealthy Cole impressed the populace with his regal, free-spending ways. Later, he gave the

Daily Express

NO. 3,071. LONDON, SATURDAY, FEBRUARY 12, 1910. ONE HALFPENNY.

TO-DAY'S STORY.

SATURDAY MORNING.

TARIFF REFORM MEANS THE HOPE OF THE WORKERS.

THE CABINET DILEMMA.

MINISTERS FACED BY NEW PERPLEXING PROBLEM.

THE IRISH BOMB.

JUGGLING WITH THE VETO BILL.

By A UNIONIST M.P.

SURPRISE FOR THE SOCIALISTS.

MR. HENDERSON RESIGNS FROM THE COMMITTEE.

WILD PROPOSALS.

DISASTER AT SEA.

MAIL STEAMER LOST AND 158 PERSONS DROWNED.

ONLY ONE SURVIVOR

PROTECTION FOR BARONETS.

PLAN TO SAFEGUARD THEIR TITLES.

ROYAL ORDER.

SULTAN IN A FURY.

MULAI HAFID ORDERS ENVOY FROM HIS PRESENCE.

TROUBLE AHEAD.

NO OLYMPIC GAMES.

ATHENS ATHLETIC FESTIVAL STOPPED BY THE CRISIS.

BEST MEN FAIL.

DR. JAMESON SAYS PROGRESSIVES MUST NOW FIGHT.

TRAINING SHIP EXPLOSION.

FIVE MEN BADLY SCALDED BY STEAM.

ROMANCE AFTER TRAGEDY

COUNTESS LINDA MURRI MARRIED IN ITALY.

ROOSEVELT ROMANCE

EX-PRESIDENT'S ELDEST SON ENGAGED TO BE MARRIED.

LORD CHARLES BERESFORD.

HEROIC BOATMAN ROBBED.

SEINE STILL RISING.

M. FALLIERES' HEALTH.

KING GUSTAF.

THE KING'S HOLIDAY DISTURBED.

CROWDS WHO DISREGARD HIS WISH FOR PRIVACY.

EARLY MORNING STROLL

ROYAL VISIT TO BROADSTAIRS.

ROYAL POETS.

VERSES BY THE MIKADO AND HIS EMPRESS.

AMAZING NAVAL HOAX.

SHAM ABYSSINIAN PRINCES VISIT THE DREADNOUGHT.

BOGUS ORDER.

MAKALIN, MENDAX AND SUITE.

PERTINENT ENQUIRIES.

WONDERFUL MAKE-UP.

SPLENDID RECEPTION.

SHOWN EVERYTHING.

story to the *Daily Mail* – a boast that almost got him expelled.

Cole's best-known feat was the *Dreadnought* Affair of 1910, which Adrian Stephen described in a 1936 book published by his sister Virginia and her husband, Leonard Woolf. The hoaxee was the Royal Navy. The perpetrators were Cole; Adrian and Virginia Stephen; Guy Ridley; Duncan Grant, the artist; and Anthony Buxton, who became a writer and naturalist. Once again, they impersonated exotic dignitaries from the East, this time, the Emperor of Ethiopia and three princes. Cole played the part of a Foreign Office official and Ridley was an interpreter.

The *Dreadnought*, flagship of the Home Fleet, was anchored at Weymouth when its commander received a telegram, purportedly from the Foreign Office, advising the arrival of the Ethiopian emperor and his suite on the 4:20 train from London. Meanwhile, the imposters went to Clarkson's, a theatrical costumer in London, where the four Ethiopians dressed up in long, elaborate robes, turbans, and beards, with dark stage make-up on their hands and faces. Virginia Stephen had cut her hair short for the occasion, and the quartet looked much like the Wise Men in a Christmas pageant. The whole party pored over a Swahili grammar, unaware that Amharic, not Swahili, was the language of Ethiopia. Fortunately, the Royal Navy knew as little about it as they did.

The imposters were both scared and excited to find a naval officer in dress uniform saluting to them as they stepped off the train from Paddington Station. A red carpet had been laid out and a barrier erected to keep sightseers at a distance. The officer drove them to the harbor and a launch took them out to the ship. There they were received by the Commander-in-Chief Home Fleet, Admiral Sir William May. They inspected a marine guard of honor, while Stephen "interpreted" the admiral's explanations in a mixture of Swahili, pig Latin, and passages from Homer, mispronounced enough to be unrecognizable as Greek.

The royal entourage exclaimed with delight and enthusiasm as they toured the ship. "Bunga bunga!" they cried appreciatively, while Virginia Stephen chimed in sotte voce, "Chuck-a-choi, chuck-a-choi." The naval officers were pleased with their childlike reactions to the sight of an electric light. The only bad moment occurred when Adrian Stephen found himself standing near his first cousin, a staff officer on the *Dreadnought*. Fortunately, he went unrecognized, despite his height (six feet, five inches, plus a top hat) and the fact that his only disguise was a moustache.

At evening, a light rain set in and the imposters made a hasty departure, concerned that their make-up and moustaches would be washed away. As usual, Cole couldn't keep the prank to himself. The whole story appeared in the *Daily Express* the following weekend. There were angry rumblings from

ABOVE: Novelist Virginia Woolf, one of the participants in the *Dreadnought* Affair.

LEFT: The front page of the *Daily Express* newspaper, dated February 12, 1910, containing an account of the *Dreadnought* Affair in the right-hand column, under the headline "Amazing Naval Hoax."

BELOW: The perpetrators of the *Dreadnought* Affair in full regalia, ready to impersonate the Emperor of Ethiopia and his entourage. Virginia Woolf is seated at the left.

the First Lord of the Admiralty and opposition leaders who wished to embarrass the government, but no repercussions for the hoaxers. The public found it all a great joke, and "Bunga, bunga!" became a stock phrase in London and Weymouth for months to come.

Another famous British hoaxer was Professor R. V. Jones, who eventually taught physics at Aberdeen University. He was famous for his practical jokes at Oxford, but he put his talents to serious use during World War II, when he deceived the Nazis repeatedly through his defense work. During the Battle of Britain, in 1940, when he was 28 years old, he discovered that the Germans were using pairs of directional radio beams to guide their night bombers to British targets. The bombers flew along one beam, guided by radio signals, until they reached the point of intersection with the second beam, over the target.

He convinced Prime Minister Winston Churchill, who ordered detector planes sent up to verify the young scientist's theory. The beams were exactly where Jones had predicted they would be. Rather than jamming the beams, Jones figured out a way to duplicate them and misdirect the Germans. The enemy planes ended up bombing

empty fields far from London in what came to be known as "the battle of the beams."

Jones was also successful in fooling German defensive radar with metal foil and various other imaginative decoys during the Allied air offensive against Germany. "Imagine," he chortled, "being told to play a joke for your country. And being given unlimited resources to do it."

The most elaborate deception of World War II was the one designed to mislead the Germans about the location of the Allied invasion of France: D-Day. Early in 1944, the complex plan to make the Germans pinpoint the Pas de Calais rather than Normandy as the Allied landing place went into play. Radio signals were concentrated in southeastern England, nearest to the Pas de Calais, as if large forces were stationed there. Double agents reported to the Germans that surveys were being made there and rail troop transport arranged to Dover and other southeastern ports.

Skillful models were designed by officers like Major Basil Spence (later the architect of Coventry Cathedral). They included balsawood gliders, inflatable tanks and landing craft, and dummy buildings visible from the air. Vehicle tracks led into the forests of Kent at various points. As a result, on June 6, the

BELOW: Prime Minister Winston Churchill pictured in 1944 signing an agreement between Dominion premiers. Churchill supported Professor R. V. Jones's attempts to foil the German Luftwaffe during World War II.

first day of the Normandy invasion, German strategists still believed that the real assault was to come later.

German Intelligence reported in early June: "The forces employed comprise only a relatively small portion of the troops available. Of the 60 large formations in southern England [in fact, there were only 35], only 10 to 12 divisions, including airborne troops, appear to be participating so far. . . . The indications are that further large-scale operations are planned." As a result, critical German forces were held back to deal with a second invasion that never materialized. It was a hoax that changed the course of history.

THIS PAGE: An inflatable tank (top) and (above) balsawood "artillery" which, from the air, were indistinguishable from the real thing.

CHAPTER TWO

PATENT MEDICINE MEN

It's possible that patent medicines came to America on the *Mayflower*, but it wasn't until the 1870s that such remedies as Hostetter's Celebrated Stomach Bitters and Lydia E. Pinkham's Vegetable Compound became household names across the land. By 1905 Samuel Hopkins Adams could write in *Collier's Weekly*: "Gullible America will spend this year some 75 millions of dollars in the purchase of patent medicines. . . . It will swallow huge quantities of alcohol, an appalling amount of opiates and narcotics, a wide assortment of varied drugs ranging from powerful and dangerous heart depressants to insidious liver stimulants; and, far in excess of all other ingredients, undiluted fraud."

The heyday of patent medicines was inseparable from the development of aggressive, widespread advertising and of trademarks that would become familiar to generations of purchasers. The ingredients of these proprietary drugs – alcohol and all – were almost interchangeable, but the reassuring Quaker on the label of Dr. Flint's Quaker Bitters and the motherly visage of Lydia Pinkham were never duplicated.

Until recently, no government agency regulated the patent-medicine makers, so they were free to make such promises as "Instantaneous Cure!" (Lloyd's Cocaine Toothache Drops) and "The Wonder and Blessing of the Age" (Dr. Townsend's Compound Extract of Sarsaparilla). They could

put anything they liked into their nostrums without listing ingredients or proportions on the label and play on public anxiety with impunity: "It Will Cure You at Home Without Pain, Plaster or Operation!" Considering the state of the medical arts of the day, who wouldn't want to believe such a claim?

Patent medicines may not have delivered on all their promises, but they made fortunes for their inventive purveyors. The first to break into the national market was Thomas Dyott, a Philadelphia shoeshiner who developed his first line of "family remedies" in 1810. By prefixing the word "Doctor" to most of his nostrums, he set a precedent and inspired public confidence, however misplaced. Dyott's most memorable compound was Dr. Robertson's Worm Destroying Lozenges (named for an imaginary Edinburgh physician Dyott claimed was his grandfather). By 1820, business was so good that he bought the Kensington Glass Works, near Philadelphia, to manufacture his own medicine bottles. Twenty years later he was making $25,000 a year.

After the Civil War, the transcontinental railroad, lower postal rates, and expanded print media all fostered the spread of patent medicines, which became more specialized with the years. Trade cards and brochures, posters, roadside signs, and ads in almanacs, daily newspapers, and the back pages of popular novels all carried the message. Drugstores like San Francisco's C. F. Richards & Company made and advertised their own line, including Richard's Bronchial Pellets, Richard's Oriental Invigorator, Trapper's Indian Oil, and Armstrong's Pulmonary Syrup.

Anything with the name "Indian" tended to sell well, and the Kickapoo Indian Medicine Company was one of the biggest purveyors. Its medications included Kickapoo Indian Oil, Indian Salve, Indian Worm Killer, and Sagwa, an all-purpose "vegetable remedy composed of roots, herbs, barks, and leaves. Sagwa acts directly upon the Stomach and Liver, and will cure all the various symptoms of Dyspepsia, including Neuralgia, Headache, Constipation, Kidney Disease, &c."

"Female complaints and weaknesses" were the focal point of Lydia Estes Pinkham's Vegetable Compound, which sold in the millions of bottles from 1883 onward. As a young woman, Lydia had studied alternative medical theories in her liberal-minded Quaker household in Lynn, Massachusetts. There she met leading abolitionists and feminists of the day, including Frederick Douglass and the Grimké sisters of South Carolina, and began to make up herbal remedies for various ills.

After her marriage to Charles Pinkham,

ABOVE: Merritt Griffin's "Indian Salve" was marketed less elaborately than that of the Kickapoo Indian Medicine Company, but nevertheless shamelessly claimed the same efficacious qualities.

LEFT: Lydia E. Pinkham's homely face surmounts an advertisement for her famous "Vegetable Compound." This potion, first marketed in 1873, was aimed at the "Ladies of the World" and was so popular that it was still being sold worldwide in the 1940s.

she administered them to her four children and neighbors. But when the Panic of 1873 threatened the family with poverty, her growing sons suggested that her Vegetable Compound could be sold in the stores. Dan Pinkham took the lead, distributing pamphlets in New York City while the others set up a cottage industry for brewing the remedy. It was his idea to use his mother's face on the label, with the signature: "Yours for Health, Lydia E. Pinkham."

The family's next sound decision was a major commitment to advertising, beginning with the front page of the daily *Boston Herald*, purchased by Dan's brother Will for $60.00. The results were so gratifying that the family moved the business from the basement to the house next door. They

LEFT: A drawing by Harold Matthews Brett showing a typical scene at a country fair in 1908: a traveling medicine man selling his wares.

RIGHT: An 1846 drawing depicting the brutal methods of an itinerant dentist, who is here pulling a tooth while seated on a horse.

BELOW: Parker's Tonic's rather unsubtle, but doubtless effective, attempt to persuade potential customers to buy their product.

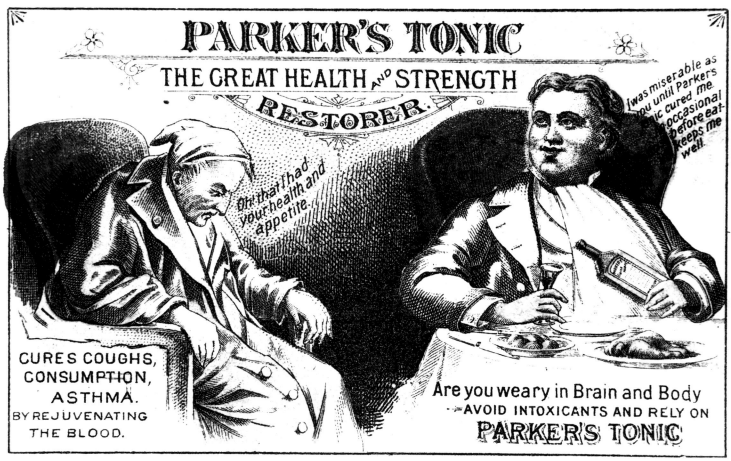

ABOVE: "The Quack
Doctor," as portrayed
in a woodcut by
F. O. C. Daley in 1871.

$300,000 a year. She had written most of the advertising and corresponded with her customers under the rubric "Write to Mrs. Pinkham." Her son Charles and daughter Aroline took over management of the business and retained James T. Wetherald to do their advertising, which he did successfully well into the twentieth century. By the 1940s, Lydia E. Pinkham was sold in 33 countries.

Like the word "Indian," "vegetable" inspired confidence, with its suggestion of tried-and-true herbal cures and remedies. Other vegetable compounds of the day included Purely Vegetable Taraxacum (Dandelion) Bitters and Paine's Celery Compound, which touched off a craze for celery remedies. These included, by the turn of the century, Celery Bitters, Celery-Cola, and Sears, Roebuck's own Celery Malt Compound and many others.

In 1912, the American Medical Association published the first in a three-volume series entitled *Nostrums and Quackery*, which exposed such remedies as Marjorie Hamilton's Obesity Cure; it included bath salts that were supposed to dissolve fat while the patient soaked in the tub. Muckraking journalists and the emerging pharmaceutical industry, which dealt in prescription (called "ethical") drugs, got into the act to denounce the abuses that were rampant. But their warnings were almost drowned out by the colorful pitchmen and pageantry of the great traveling medicine shows, which had been going strong since the late 1800s.

The traveling medicine show combined elements of the circus, the Revival meeting, and the theater, and proved irresistible to the "rubes" who turned out for the rare treat of professional entertainment. (It would be decades before the term "snake oil salesman" was used for phony pitchman of all kinds.) Most patent medicine men borrowed the title of "Doctor" and appeared in frock coats and top hats to lend dignity to the occasion.

"Shills" were planted in the audience to buy the first bottle of medicine and pretend they had been cured of some long-standing affliction. One of the most celebrated pitchmen of his day was William Avery "Doc" Rockefeller who traveled the Midwest after the Civil War. His story is told by David Armstrong and Elizabeth Metzger Armstrong in *The Great American Medicine Show*, published by Prentice-Hall in 1991:

"Rockefeller peddled packaged herbs and billed himself as 'the Celebrated Cancer Specialist.' He sold his cancer cure for the then-stupendous sum of 25 dollars and was known as a good storyteller who played a mean banjo. Leaving his wife and soon-to-

capitalized on the fact that the compound was "home-brewed" and noted that the alcohol content (some 18 percent) was "used only as a solvent and preservative."

By the time Lydia died in 1883, her Vegetable Compound was bringing in some

ABOVE: The association between Native American tradition and patent medicine appeared a magically successful combination, and medicine men continued to link the two well into the twentieth century. Here an "Indian" medicine man tries to interest a Tennessee farmhand in his panacea in 1945.

LEFT: John D. Rockefeller pictured with his family. The father of this famous philanthropist was a bigamist and notorious quack pitchman, William Avery "Doc" Rockefeller, whose speciality was a cancer "cure."

be-famous son, John D. Rockefeller, behind, Doc lived in a bigamous marriage in South Dakota as Dr. William Levingston. Although relations between father and son were understandably strained, John D. never entirely rejected the influence of Doctor Bill. Indeed, the petroleum mogul took patent medicines for his health long after the family business changed from snake oil to Standard Oil.''

As time went on, the biggest manufacturers set up their own medicine shows, including John A. Hamlin, producer of Hamlin's Wizard Oil, ''the great medical conqueror.'' His trademark was an elephant ridden by a turbaned man who lent the whole enterprise an Oriental flavor. In fact, many patent medicines borrowed mystery and glamour from the Far East, as seen in such products as Dr. Drake's Canton Chinese Hair Cream, Persian Balm, and Westphalia Stomach Bitters. Medicine woman Violet McNeal sometimes appeared as the Oriental healer Lotus Blossom.

The Society of Friends was plagued by the number of pitchmen who traded on the Quaker's reputation for honesty by dressing in modest clothes and wearing low-crowned hats when they hawked their wares. Quakers appeared on bottles of liniment and cathartic pills. A pitchman who called himself Brother John made his rounds

in a horse-drawn chariot and pulled teeth in his spare time, like the medicine-show dentist who would become well known as Painless Parker. (A famous publicity shot shows Parker working on the incisors of a hippopotamus, perhaps drugged for the occasion.)

The American Indians' reputation as a noble savage led to all kinds of exploitation by the patent-medicine makers. The Kickapoo Indian Medicine Company published a full-length illustrated book called *Life and Scenes Among the Kickapoo Indians: Their Manners, Habits and Customs*. In among the staged scenes of ''Indian Life in a Kickapoo Village'' were numerous ads for the company's line. Kickapoo Salve had a picture of a bison on its tin, creating some confusion about whether the Kickapoos were Eastern or Western Plains Indians. In fact, half of those who traveled with the show weren't Indians at all.

The company had been founded in 1881 by two men named John E. Healy, originally a salesman of King of Pain liniment, and ''Texas Charlie'' Bigelow, who was as close as the company ever got to the real Kickapoo nation residing in Oklahoma Territory. Its headquarters, called the Principal Wigwam, was near New Haven, Connecticut. The firm's best-known remedy was Indian Sagwa, primarily a laxative but also touted as a cure for dyspepsia, rheumatism, and

LEFT: John D. Rockefeller was responsible for changing the nature of the family business from snake oil to Standard Oil, as advertised here.

BELOW: A poster celebrating William Cody's Wild West Show. Buffalo Bill was persuaded to endorse the Kickapoo Indian Medicine Company's ''Indian Sagwa'' with the help of a mythical Native American princess who rejoiced in the healthy name of Little Bright Eye.

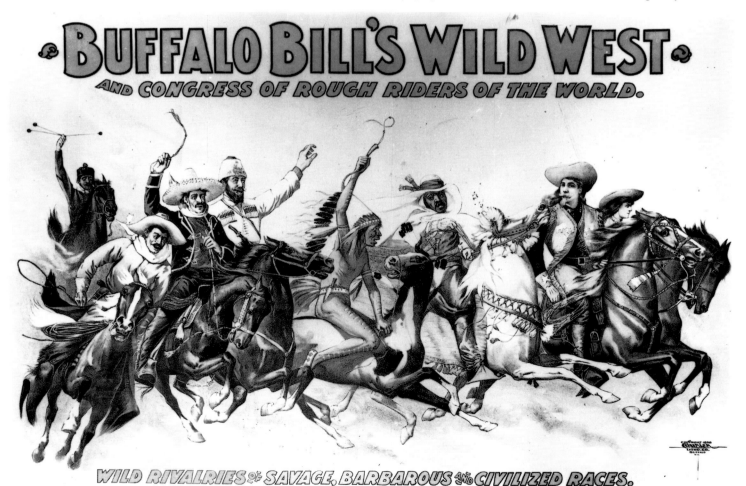

other ills. It was claimed that Texas Charlie had discovered Sagwa when he was nursed back to health from a near-fatal prairie fever by an Indian family. The Western theme was carried out by employing Buffalo Bill Cody to endorse the product, along with a mythical Indian Princess called Little Bright Eye.

Several famous Americans, including P. T. Barnum and the poet James Whitcomb Riley, did stints with the medicine shows or wrote copy for the medicine men. Barnum touted a cure for baldness, and Riley provided musical and poetic accompaniment for Dr. C. M. Townsend, who went on the road with his Cholera Balm and King of Cough medicine. A doctor named N. T. Oliver took the stage name of "Nevada Ned" to run shows for Healy and Bigelow as well as John A. Hamlin. He did some trick shooting in the Wild West-style shows and wrote crime novels on the side. Nevada Ned once took a Kickapoo show with over 100 members – perhaps the largest ever mounted – to Chicago, where a major newspaper sent a critic to review it.

Dr. Painless Parker was – a rarity at the time – a licensed dentist who was born Edgar Randolph Parker in the Canadian Maritimes. He spent his entire career practicing "theatrical dentistry" all over North America. He injected his patients with hydrocain, a forerunner of novocaine, which made it easier to do street-corner extractions than ether, which was the major anaesthetic of the day. Ether put subjects into a deep sleep.

Even when Parker opened a conventional office in Brooklyn, he mounted four-story signs on Flatbush Avenue proclaiming "I am positively IT in painless dentistry!" Tightrope walkers teetered between Parker's building and the ones across the street, and a small brass band played outside.

When this humdrum practice became too boring, Parker moved to Los Angeles, where he started the Parker Dental Circus. A West Coast magazine wrote a feature on it, taking particular notice of the tattooed lady, the living skeleton, and the giant molar surprinted with Parker's portrait. The bandstand was built to resemble an open mouth, which must have been unnerving for the musicians.

Parker finally sold the circus and went into semi-retirement, emerging to blow his cornet and pull teeth in San Francisco streets because he missed the crowds. He had become a rich man, with a chain of 28 dental offices and the biggest yacht in San Francisco Bay. *The Great American Medicine Show* reports that *Collier's* magazine photographed Parker for a three-part series shortly before his death in 1952: "Around

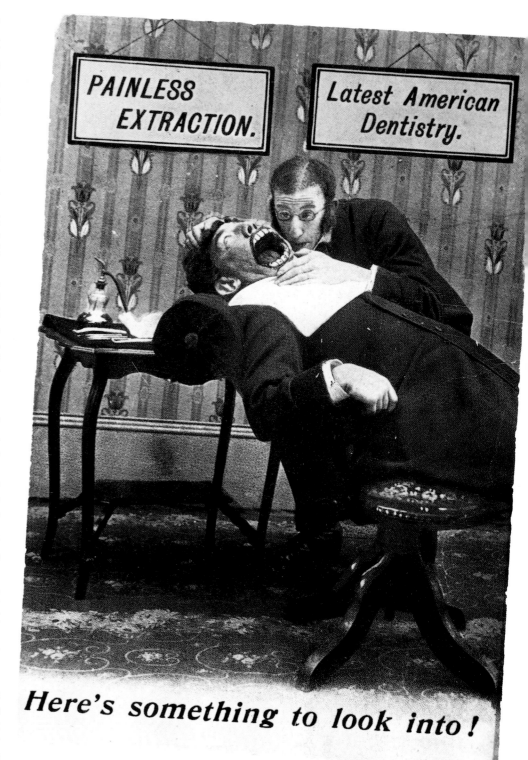

his neck was a necklace of 357 teeth. Parker had pulled them all in one wild day in 1905, near Poughkeepsie, New York."

The medicine shows began to lose their momentum in the early 1900s, although they continued into the 1940s. Federal regulation, radio and movies, and the great migration to the cities all played a part in their demise. As Thomas Kelley, owner of the Shamrock Medicine Show, had prophesied mournfully well before the end: "The natives are wiser now, here, there, and everywhere in North America. Soon there will be no such thing as a rube."

ABOVE: This humorous postcard dating from 1905 is a good illustration of the ubiquitous dental buzzword – "Painless." The most celebrated dentist was Dr. "Painless" Parker, founder of the Parker Dental Circus.

LEFT: William Cody – Buffalo Bill – pictured leaning on a rifle.

PEN NAMES AND MISNOMERS

PAGE 48: England's
Charles I was the
subject of a
seventeenth-century
hoax when pro-
monarchy clergyman
John Gauden
published a journal
purported to be by the
executed king.

ABOVE: The frontispiece
of John Gauden's
faked journal known as
the *Eikon Basilike*
which put the executed
king in a favorable light.

Literary deceptions are as old as the written word and have become more prevalent as writers acquired more social status and pay. The great library at Alexandria, one of the wonders of the ancient world, had its share of frauds and forgeries in the names of Aristotle and Euripedes. Renaissance poets and Elizabethan dramatists had their wistful imitators. Today, the huge sums commanded by celebrity biographies inspire literary larceny on a grand scale.

Propaganda motives have given rise to such fakes as the seventeenth century *Eikon Basilike*, which was published as the journal of Charles I shortly after he was executed by Cromwell's party. A Royalist clergyman named John Gauden wrote it to put the deceased king in a favorable light and incite hostility against the Cromwellians. The book was instrumental in the restoration of the monarchy, and Gauden was made Bishop of Exeter as a result.

Another famous literary forgery was Charles Julius Bertram's history and topography of Roman Britain, which he claimed to have found. It was accompanied by a detailed map and attributed to the fourteenth-century historian Richard of Cirencester. The book was published to scholarly acclaim and cited as a reference for 100 years. Royal Ordnance Survey maps listed the locations on Bertram's map, until the book was denounced as a fraud late in the nineteenth century.

One of the saddest stories in the history of *noms de plume* is that of 17-year-old Thomas Chatterton, an aspiring poet of the late eighteenth century. Lacking confidence in the series of romantic poems he had written, he rewrote them in Old English

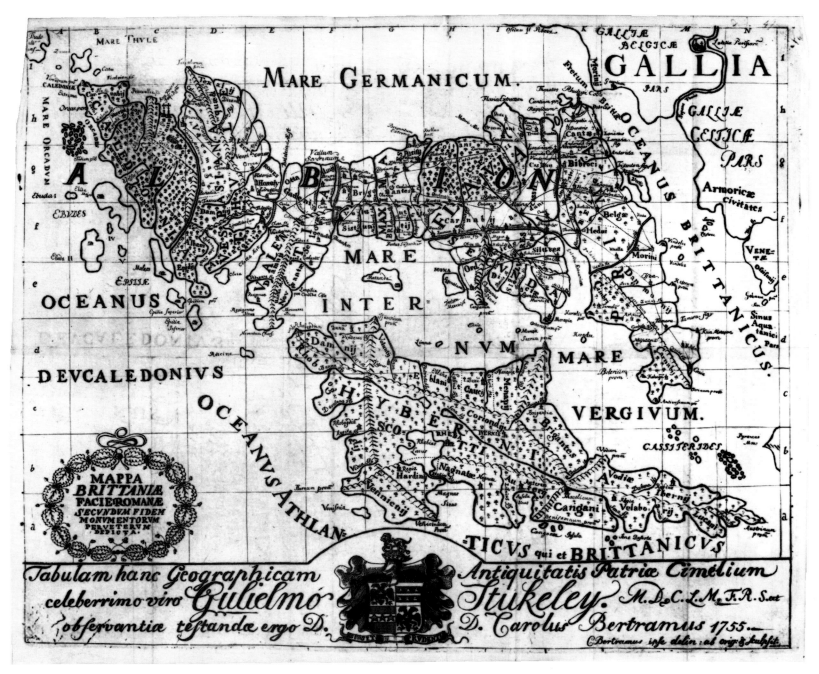

MARE GERMANICUM.

GALLIA

OCEANUS

DEUCALEDONIUS

OCEANUS ATHLAN-

MARE INTER- -NUM MARE

VERGIVUM.

MAPPA
BRITTANIÆ
FACIEROMANÆ
SECVNDVM FIDEM
MONVMENTORVM
PERVETERVM
DEPICTA

TICVS qui et BRITTANICVS

Tabulam hanc Geographicam   Antiquitatis Patriæ Cimelium
celeberrimo viro Gulielmó   Stukeley. M.DCL.MF.R.Sat
observantiæ testandæ ergo D.   D. Carolus Bertramus 1755.

ABOVE: A map attributed to the fourteenth-century historian Richard of Cirencester in Charles Julius Bertram's bogus work on the history and topography of Roman Britain.

LEFT: Part of the frontispiece of Bertram's spoof book based on the wholly fabricated works of the non-existent Richard of Cirencester.

and brought them out as the work of Thomas Rowley, a medieval monk. Author and critic Horace Walpole discovered their true origin and exposed the young poet to denunciation as a fraud.

Chatterton committed suicide, and the poetry's true merit was recognized only after his death. Walpole himself had begun his literary career with a deception, when he published his novel *The Castle of Otranto* (1764) as a translation from the Italian of a manuscript alleged to be 200 years old. Only after the novel was successful did he republish it under his own name (with apologies to his readers).

Young William Henry Ireland became a forger of letters, poems, and a play attributed to William Shakespeare, not for money, but to win the approval of his father. Samuel Ireland, an artist and antiquarian bookseller, paid scant attention to his son, who was expelled from school for lack of in-

ABOVE: An example of one of William Henry Ireland's many forgeries of material supposedly relating to the life and works of William Shakespeare.

LEFT: Henry Wallis's painting of the self-inflicted death of Chatterton, the young, late eighteenth-century poet who created Old English verse which he attributed to Thomas Rowley, a medieval monk.

LEFT: A page from the faked romantic verse credited to Thomas Rowley but in fact the work of aspiring poet Thomas Chatterton.

LEFT: English wit and author Horace Walpole (1717-1797) exposed the fakery of the young Chatterton and helped to precipitate his suicide. Ironically, Walpole himself was involved in trickery when he published his own novel *The Castle of Otranto* as the translation of a 200-year-old Italian book.

BELOW LEFT: The young William Henry Ireland, who embarked on a career of literary forgery to satisfy his father's fascination with the great William Shakespeare.

BELOW: An example of Chatterton's attempts to master the intricacies of medieval writing before he began his Rowley forgeries.

telligence. However on leaving his home environment for a French boarding school, the boy did much better at his studies and determined to win his father's esteem.

In 1793, the 17-year-old Ireland accompanied his father to Stratford-upon-Avon, Shakespeare's birthplace, which was then becoming a literary shrine. The elder Ireland was carried away by his enthusiasm for the immortal bard. He bought several relics of dubious origin and expressed his deep desire to add a manuscript of Shakespeare's to his collection.

When the pair returned to London, William Henry was apprenticed to a lawyer, but his dream was to produce a document of Shakespeare's to please his father. He set to work on the project with an old piece of parchment and a bottle of ink made up to give the look of antiquity.

William's first forgery was a title deed to property near the Globe Theatre, signed with Shakespeare's name and that of the alleged seller. To account for his possession of the deed, he told his father that he had met a wealthy country gentleman in a coffee house who offered to show him his collection of old papers and documents. When William discovered the deed, "Mr. H.," as he called himself, told him he was welcome to take it if he would keep his own name out of the matter. Samuel Ireland was overjoyed to have such a relic of his literary hero, which he had authenticated by a well-known scholar. Naturally, William offered to find more material.

Soon two more pieces of Shakespeariana appeared in the family bookstore: a letter about the real estate transaction and a receipt to Shakespeare from the actor John Hemynge, written in faultless Elizabethan English. They attracted so much attention that William was inspired to produce a copy of a letter from Shakespeare to the Earl of Southampton, thanking him for his patronage. James Boswell, the biographer of Samuel Johnson, knelt down and kissed the manuscript in homage.

Urged on by his father, William revisited the mysterious Mr. H. and got permission to search his country house for additional treasures. In short order, he came up with a love poem to Anne Hathaway, marginal notes in Shakespeare's hand to books from his personal library, and a letter to the playwright from Queen Elizabeth herself. By now, the Prince of Wales had joined the visitors to Samuel Ireland's shop off The Strand in London.

William's confidence was growing fast, and soon he overreached himself. He came up with original manuscripts for *King Lear* and *Hamlet* which he edited, deleting some ribald passages and changing several lines.

But rather than exciting suspicion, the manuscripts were well received, with one critic applauding the "straight, manly style" of William's versions. The next step was obvious: the discovery of a full-length play that had never been published.

William's subject was the Anglo-Saxon king Vortigern; he used Hollinghead's *Chronicles*, the source of many Shakespearean plots, for his *Vortigern and Rowena*. The style bore comparison in some passages to Shakespeare's flights of imagery, but much of it was contrived and wooden, the iambic pentameter monotonous in its effect.

Since the forgery of a five-act Elizabethan-style play would involve incredible labor, William told his father that Mr. H. had let him copy it out from the original. Richard Sheridan, then owner of the Drury Lane Theatre, agreed to produce the play, although he found some of it "crude and undigested." "It is very odd," wrote Sheridan. "One would be led to believe that Shakespeare must have been very young when he wrote the play."

ABOVE, FAR LEFT: Passed off as a Shakespearean self-portrait, this is in fact the work of William Henry Ireland.

ABOVE: London's Drury Lane Theatre was the venue for the production of Ireland's bogus Shakespearean play *Vortigern and Rowena*.

FAR LEFT: James Boswell as painted by Sir Joshua Reynolds. Boswell, a leading literary figure, was fooled by Ireland's forgeries.

LEFT: Richard Sheridan, owner of Drury Lane, agreed to stage *Vortigern and Rowena*.

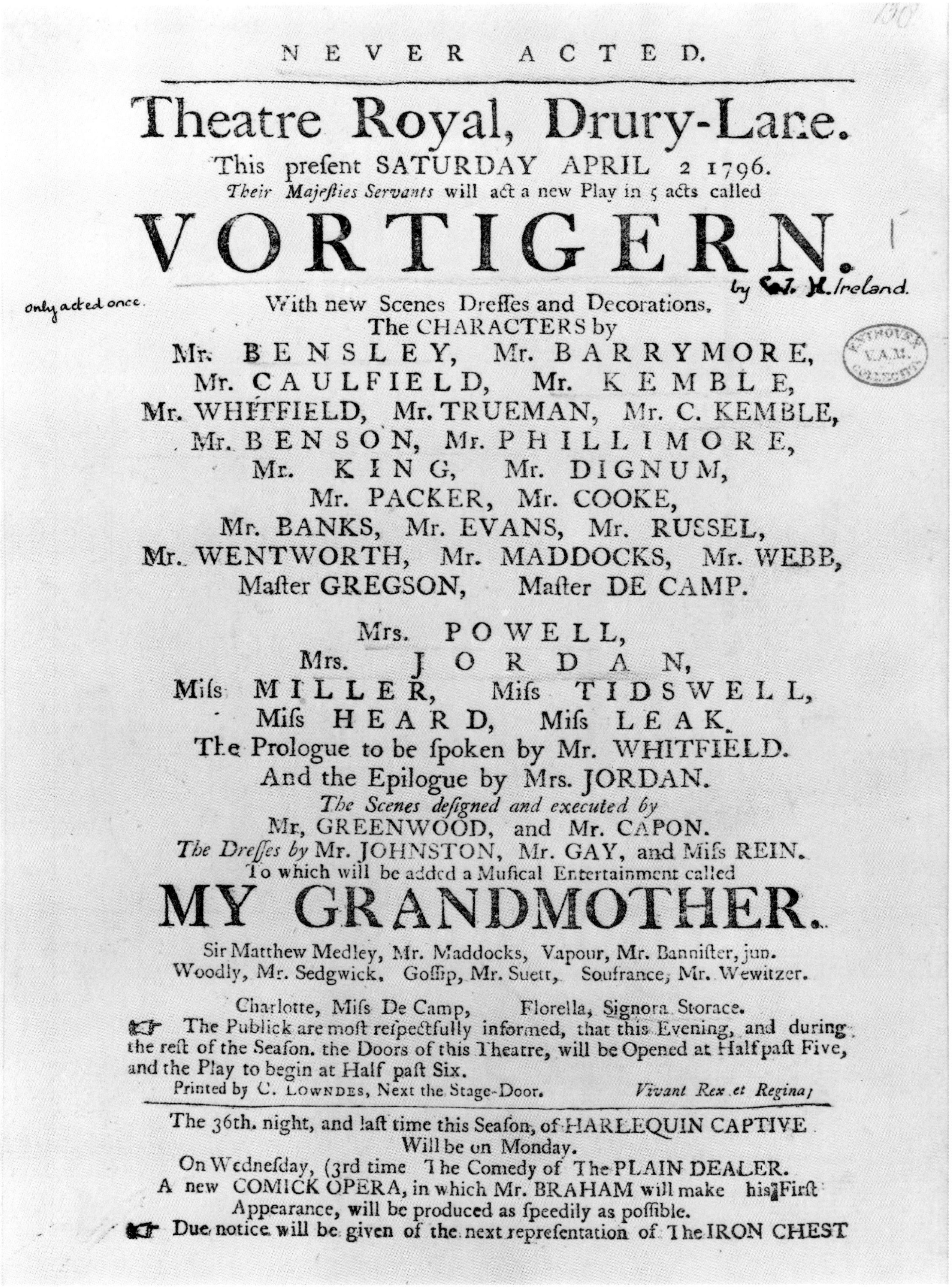

130

NEVER ACTED.

Theatre Royal, Drury-Lane.

This prefent SATURDAY APRIL 2 1796.
Their Majefties Servants will act a new Play in 5 acts called

VORTIGERN.

by W. H. Ireland

only acted once.

With new Scenes Dreffes and Decorations,
The CHARACTERS by
Mr. BENSLEY, Mr. BARRYMORE,
Mr. CAULFIELD, Mr. KEMBLE,
Mr. WHITFIELD, Mr. TRUEMAN, Mr. C. KEMBLE,
Mr. BENSON, Mr. PHILLIMORE,
Mr. KING, Mr. DIGNUM,
Mr. PACKER, Mr. COOKE,
Mr. BANKS, Mr. EVANS, Mr. RUSSEL,
Mr. WENTWORTH, Mr. MADDOCKS, Mr. WEBB,
Mafter GREGSON, Mafter DE CAMP.

Mrs. POWELL,
Mrs. JORDAN,
Mifs MILLER, Mifs TIDSWELL,
Mifs HEARD, Mifs LEAK.
The Prologue to be fpoken by Mr. WHITFIELD.
And the Epilogue by Mrs. JORDAN.
The Scenes defigned and executed by
Mr. GREENWOOD, and Mr. CAPON.
The Dreffes by Mr. JOHNSTON, Mr. GAY, and Mifs REIN.
To which will be added a Mufical Entertainment called

MY GRANDMOTHER.

Sir Matthew Medley, Mr. Maddocks, Vapour, Mr. Bannifter, jun.
Woodly, Mr. Sedgwick, Goffip, Mr. Suett, Soufrance, Mr. Wewitzer.

Charlotte, Mifs De Camp, Florella, Signora Storace.
☞ The Publick are moft refpectfully informed, that this Evening, and during
the reft of the Seafon. the Doors of this Theatre, will be Opened at Half paft Five,
and the Play to begin at Half paft Six.
Printed by C. LOWNDES, Next the Stage-Door. *Vivant Rex et Regina;*

The 36th. night, and laft time this Seafon, of HARLEQUIN CAPTIVE
Will be on Monday.
On Wednefday, (3rd time The Comedy of The PLAIN DEALER.
A new COMICK OPERA, in which Mr. BRAHAM will make his First
Appearance, will be produced as fpeedily as poffible.
☞ Due notice will be given of the next reprefentation of The IRON CHEST

Unfortunately, *Vortigern and Rowena* was a debacle that survived only one performance, and critics who had become suspicious of the Ireland manuscripts became outspoken in describing them as fakes. Young William found that he had put his father in a false position, and he finally confessed to him what he had done – only to be disbelieved. Samuel Ireland had a deep vested interest in the Shakespeare documents, and he flatly denied that his son could have produced them. He even published *Vortigern and Rowena* and William's last forgery, *William IV*, in 1799. He was still defending their authenticity on his deathbed.

The Scottish poet James McPherson sought fame with the eighteenth-century epic poems *Fingal* and *Temora*, which he attributed to a third-century Highland bard named Ossian. McPherson claimed that the poems had come down through the centuries by tradition and that they were first published in Gaelic. To prove it, he published several Gaelic texts that he claimed to have translated into English. (The epics were, in fact, drawn from old legends.) Most critics of the day were taken in; they praised the work in glowing terms. It was compared to the Greek classics and

translated into many European languages. The deception was discovered long after McPherson's burial in Westminster Abbey, the last resting place of Britain's literary lions.

American history is full of literary frauds and legends that became history because they were repeated so often and so solemnly. The tale of Betsy Ross and the first American flag is as dubious as that of George Washington and the cherry tree. But where is the middle-aged American who didn't hear these stories in grade school as sober fact?

Another mythologized figure is naval hero John Paul Jones, whose best-known nineteenth-century biographer was Augustus C. Buell. His book was filled with errors, as pointed out in 1906 by a critic named de Koven. Buell's biography not only misattributed Jones's surname to an imaginary William Jones, it included a list of references that was wholly imaginary. No such books or authors existed.

To compound the problem, Alfred Henry Lewis wrote his own biography of Jones using Buell's book as his only source. When he was congratulated on the authenticity of his version, as compared to Buell's, he asserted, "I just took it [Buell's biography] and

ABOVE: "The Goldmines of Ireland," a contemporary print, ridiculing the discovery of William Henry Ireland's "new" Shakespearean manuscripts.

FAR LEFT: A playbill advertising the performance of Ireland's faked play.

BELOW: John Paul Jones, the U.S. naval hero, whose life story was forged by Augustus C. Buell.

FAR LEFT: *The Shadow of the Heroes Who Died Before Ossian* by Anne-Louis Girodet-Trioson. The works of Ossian, a noted literary forgery, were created by Scottish hoaxer James McPherson in the eighteenth century.

LEFT: Westminster Abbey in London, the last resting place of the country's literary greats, was the last resting place of the con artist James McPherson.

BELOW: The fake biography of John Paul Jones by Augustus Buell was, unusually, used as a major source for a second work on the naval hero by Alfred Henry Lewis.

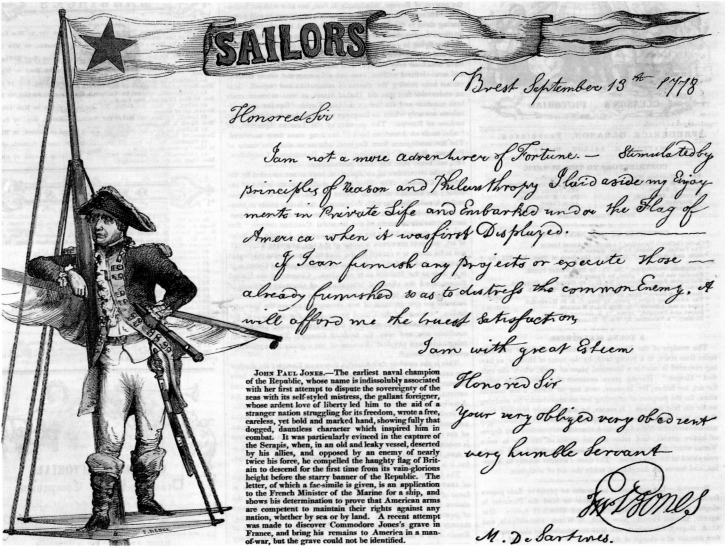

SAILORS

Brest September 13th 1778

Honored Sir

I am not a mere adventurer of Fortune. — Stimulated by principles of Reason and Philanthropy I laid aside my Enjoyments in Private Life and Embarked under the Flag of America when it was first Displayed. —

If I can furnish any projects or execute those — already furnished so as to distress the common Enemy, it will afford me the truest Satisfaction.

I am with great Esteem

Honored Sir

Your very obliged very obedient very humble Servant

J P Jones

M. D. Sartines.

JOHN PAUL JONES.—The earliest naval champion of the Republic, whose name is indissolubly associated with her first attempt to dispute the sovereignty of the seas with its self-styled mistress, the gallant foreigner, whose ardent love of liberty led him to the aid of a stranger nation struggling for its freedom, wrote a free, careless, yet bold and marked hand, showing fully that dogged, dauntless character which inspired him in combat. It was particularly evinced in the capture of the Serapis, when, in an old and leaky vessel, deserted by his allies, and opposed by an enemy of nearly twice his force, he compelled the haughty flag of Britain to descend for the first time from its vain-glorious height before the starry banner of the Republic. The letter, of which a fac-simile is given, is an application to the French Minister of the Marine for a ship, and shows his determination to prove that American arms are competent to maintain their rights against any nation, whether by sea or by land. A recent attempt was made to discover Commodore Jones's grave in France, and bring his remains to America in a man-of-war, but the grave could not be identified.

RIGHT: President Abraham Lincoln was the focal point for a scam by Wilma Frances Minor who claimed to have in her possession love letters between Lincoln and Ann Rutledge.

RIGHT: A forged sample of Lincoln's writing.

translated it into my own language. If it's all wrong, so's my book.''

Abraham Lincoln's signature has been forged more often than that of anyone else in American history. The legends about the Great Emancipator began well before his death in 1865. Most people have heard the story about how Lincoln walked miles on a winter day to return a pittance that a merchant had mistakenly given him as change. Another durable story was the one about Lincoln turning up a day late for his wedding to Mary Todd.

Theories of conspiracy surrounded his assassination by John Wilkes Booth, much like those that sprang up around John F. Kennedy's untimely death a century later. In their book *Hoaxes That Made Headlines*, Herma Silverstein and Caroline Arnold tell the story of the alleged Lincoln love letters to Ann Rutledge. It had long been speculated that this young woman, who had died of malaria in her twenties, was Lincoln's first love. During the late 1920s, when Ellery Sedgwick was the editor of *Atlantic Monthly* magazine, a San Diego newspaper

BELOW: The memorial marking the final resting place of Ann Rutledge, alleged to have been Abraham Lincoln's first love.

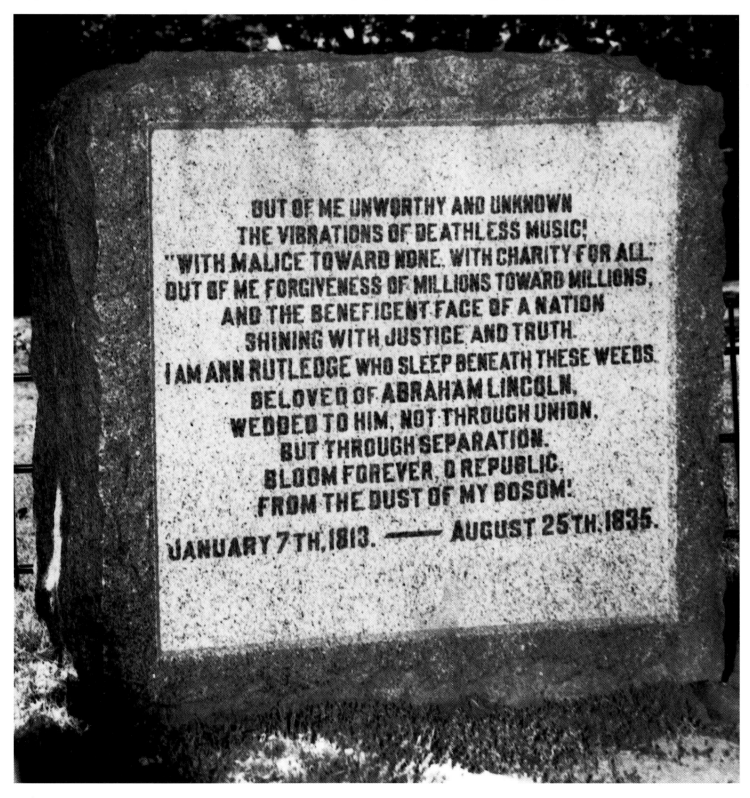

OUT OF ME UNWORTHY AND UNKNOWN
THE VIBRATIONS OF DEATHLESS MUSIC;
"WITH MALICE TOWARD NONE, WITH CHARITY FOR ALL."
OUT OF ME FORGIVENESS OF MILLIONS TOWARD MILLIONS,
AND THE BENEFICENT FACE OF A NATION
SHINING WITH JUSTICE AND TRUTH.
I AM ANN RUTLEDGE WHO SLEEP BENEATH THESE WEEDS,
BELOVED OF ABRAHAM LINCOLN,
WEDDED TO HIM, NOT THROUGH UNION,
BUT THROUGH SEPARATION.
BLOOM FOREVER, O REPUBLIC,
FROM THE DUST OF MY BOSOM.
JANUARY 7TH, 1813. ——— AUGUST 25TH, 1835.

columnist named Wilma Frances Minor offered to sell the prestigious journal a collection of Lincoln love letters and related documents for $5000.

She claimed that the material had come down to her mother's family, the De Boyers, and contained information about Lincoln's personal life that had never been published. Sedgwick was so interested that he promised a $1000 advance for the letters and published the following announcement in the December 1928 issue: "At last, after nearly a century, appear the priceless documents which lift the veil shrouding the love affair between Abraham Lincoln and young Ann Rutledge."

At the same time, Sedgwick asked a famous Lincoln scholar, the Reverend William E. Barton, to authenticate the collection. It included romantic correspondence between the future president and his alleged first love; the diary of Matilda Cameron, Ann's cousin and intimate; letters from Lincoln to his mentor politician John Calhoun; a statement from Calhoun's daughter Sally; and books annotated and signed by Lincoln.

Barton was highly skeptical – until he met Miss Minor. Her charm and plausibility made him a believer. Poet and Lincoln biographer Carl Sandburg gave his opinion that "these new letters seem entirely authentic." But historian Paul A. Angle warned Sedgwick, after testing the letters' paper, ink, and handwriting, that they were fraudulent. He was disregarded in an excess of editorial optimism, and the first article in the series "Lincoln the Lover" appeared soon afterward.

The literate readers of *Atlantic Monthly*, and the critics, were both quick to point out that the article contained glaring errors. For one thing, the letters were signed "Abe," a nickname Lincoln hated and never used. References in a letter of 1834 to "someplace called Kansas" predated the formation of the Kansas territory by 20 years. A Rutledge letter mentioned "Spencer's copybook" on penmanship, which wasn't published until 13 years after Ann's death. Sedgwick was especially dismayed by a letter from the editor of the Massachusetts Historical Society, who declared, "You are putting over one of the crudest forgeries I have known."

Critical editorials appeared in the *New York Times* and other newspapers across the country. Eventually, even Barton and Sandburg reversed their first judgment that the letters were authentic. The circulation manager of the *Atlantic Monthly* wrote Wilma Minor to urge that she bring a lawsuit against the Reverend Barton, but Clara De Boyer wrote back to say that her daughter could not face such an ordeal. The magazine's staff was shocked to discover that her handwriting was identical to that of the Lincoln correspondence.

Sedgwick's editors pressured him into undertaking a private investigation of Wilma Minor and her mother that proved the Lincoln letters were fraudulent. In the end, Minor confessed that her mother had composed them under "spirit guidance" from Lincoln and Rutledge "so that my gifts as a writer combined with her gifts as a medium could hand in something worthwhile to the world." Neither woman was prosecuted for fraud, and an embarrassed Sedgwick withdrew the series "Lincoln the Lover" from publication.

The pseudo-glamour of the 1920s underworld inspired a profitable hoax entitled *Carrying a Gun for Al Capone*. This was allegedly the autobiography of a young German immigrant named Jack Bilbo, first published in Germany in 1930 and then translated into several languages, including English. It became a best-seller, hailed by critics as "an excellent pen portrait of Al Capone" with "dramatic glimpses into a sinister underworld."

Bilbo, born Hugo Baruch, had actually visited the United States early in his flamboyant career as a bohemian painter and adventurer, although he had never been to Chicago, where the story was set. But imagination made up for lack of experience when he described his foray into gangland. He claimed that he had served as an apprentice gunman and as one of Capone's bodyguards. He'd participated in fights, gun battles, extortion, and underworld executions. Obligingly, he posed for publicity shots in trenchcoat and snap-brim hat, with a pistol in his hand.

His description of Al Capone was almost worth the price of the book: "True, he did have a certain animal wildness in his face, but a wildness reminiscent of a wildcat rather than a gorilla. . . . His glance was piercing, strong, and a trifle sad. His nose was flat, sensual. His mouth was big and broad, and his underlip curled."

Today, it is hard to believe that this naive and overwrought prose could have been taken seriously by critics and public alike. But it appealed to the sentiments of the day, like the gritty gangster films of the 1930s. The author's previous manuscripts had been rejected by return of post, but *Carrying a Gun for Al Capone* sent publishers in pursuit of him with money in hand. When he exhibited some of his paintings in London in 1939, a British newspaper solemnly reported that he had killed at least a dozen people in his role as a Chicago gangster.

LEFT: Infamous gangster Al Capone in a publicity shot from 1930. Capone was the main topic of Jack Bilbo's highly profitable, but entirely imaginary autobiography *Carrying a Gun for Al Capone*.

BELOW: Capone's most notorious deed was the St. Valentine's Day Massacre, executed in 1929. Pictured below are policemen carrying away bodies from the scene of the crime.

One of the twentieth century's most famous literary frauds is the fake autobiography of billionaire Howard Hughes written by novelist Clifford Irving in the early 1970s. He got the idea from a news magazine story about Hughes, who had been a celebrity earlier in his life as a pioneer aviator, expert golfer, and producer of such films as *Scarface* and *Hell's Angels*. In 1939 he flew around the world in half the time set by the record-breaking Charles Lindbergh and was awarded the Congressional Medal of Honor by President Franklin D. Roosevelt.

His sudden disappearance from public life excited great speculation about him and set reporters on the trail of his former wives and business associates. But from the late 1950s, he saw no one but his personal staff. His last interview was given to *Time* magazine bureau chief Frank McCulloch in the late 1950s. It was rumored that he lived on Paradise Island in the Bahamas.

ABOVE: Actor Paul Muni as gangster Tony Camonte in *Scarface* (1931), a movie which was directly based on the shady and violent world of Al Capone.

LEFT: Billionaire Howard Hughes (with raised hand) posing for photographers in 1938. His eccentric lifestyle was a source of endless fascination to the American public.

RIGHT: Clifford Irving: a conman whose energetic ingenuity persuaded the world that he was collaborating with Howard Hughes on the latter's autobiography.

BELOW: Irving is the focus of intense interest as he arrives at the U.S. Attorney's Office in 1972, having been subpoenaed by both a Federal and a New York County grand jury.

Irving took a huge risk when he forged a letter from Howard Hughes that requested his help in writing an autobiography. This was an even bigger gamble than writing the "unauthorized biography" of someone who might sue for libel or slander. In fact, Irving has the distinction of being the only writer to fabricate a literary work by a living person. He counted on Hughes being out of touch with the world to protect him from the accusation of forgery.

Thus he convinced his publishers, McGraw-Hill, to pay him a $750,000 advance, to be split between himself and Hughes, the checks to be payable to "H. R. Hughes." Irving's wife Edith then opened a Swiss bank account in the name of Helga Renate Hughes and deposited the money. The contract also called for communication solely between author and subject, so the publishers couldn't learn that Hughes was not involved.

Irving's accomplice in the deception was his friend and associate Richard Suskind, who recorded imaginary interviews with him. When *Life* magazine expressed interest in printing excerpts from the forthcoming book, Irving gained access to its files on Hughes and photographed interviews with him that had never been published. *Life* had handwriting experts verify the authenticity of Hughes's letter to Irving, and they declared it was genuine.

The plot grew ever more complex, as Irving flew all over the world, ostensibly to meet with Hughes at remote locations. The publishers assigned codenames to author and subject to meet the condition of total secrecy about the manuscript prior to its appearance in print. Meanwhile, Edith Irving made periodic trips to Switzerland with a forged passport, disguised in a black wig, to deposit advance checks.

In mid-1971, unaware of the forgery in progress, film agent Stanley Meyer asked his friend Irving to consider rewriting a book on Howard Hughes. The manuscript had been cowritten by Hughes associate Noah

ABOVE: Edith Irving played an important role in the fraud. It was she who opened a Swiss bank account in the name of Helga Renate Hughes, in which the couple's ill-gotten gains were deposited.

Dietrich and magazine writer James Phalen. Irving took the manuscript and photocopied it, then told Meyer he wasn't interested in the project. Thus he was able to plagiarize information known only to Dietrich and Phalen.

Later that summer, Irving's editor told him that a man named Sam Post, was representing a Hughes autobiography as told to Robert Eaton, and had sold excerpts to the *Ladies Home Journal*. McGraw-Hill was under pressure to announce the book by Irving and Suskind before publication, despite the secrecy clause in the contract. Irving hastily forged another letter from Hughes giving McGraw-Hill permission to announce his autobiography at once on account of "the Eaton book hoax." (The condition was simultaneous payment of the last advance – $350,000.)

At this point, the whole plot began to unravel. No sooner did McGraw-Hill announce the book than writer James Phalen learned that it contained passages known only to Hughes's aide Noah Dietrich and himself. Whole pages of their text had been lifted bodily for the Irving/Suskind book. Phalen charged the other two with plagiarism.

Alarmed, the editors at McGraw-Hill went back to the handwriting experts for another comparison of Hughes's letter to Irving with a genuine sample of his script. The experts found evidence they had overlooked the first time; they declared that Irving's letter was a forgery. Then came news from the Credit Suisse Bank: depositor Helga R. Hughes was, in fact, Edith Irving.

Finally, Howard Hughes himself came on the scene via a tape recorded conference call with *Time*'s Frank McCulloch. Hughes told the newsman, in the hearing of six other reporters who knew his voice, that he had never met anyone named Clifford Irving, much less commissioned him to write his life story.

The three perpetrators were tried for fraud and grand larceny in the spring of 1972. Richard Suskind was sentenced to six months in prison as an accomplice to fraud. Edith Irving was fined $10,000 and sentenced to two years in prison, most of which time was served on probation. Her husband was also fined $10,000 and sentenced to two-and-one-half years in prison. Ten years later, he was allegedly still a million dollars in debt for his unauthorized autobiography of Howard Hughes.

LEFT: Noah Dietrich (left), a Hughes aide, and writer James Phalen were the *bona fide* authors of Hughes's biography.

RIGHT: Irving's original manuscript is auctioned off in Houston in 1989.

ABOVE: German historian Dr. Werner Maser peruses his publication *Hitler's Letters and Notes.* Maser himself was not without notoriety, having claimed in 1977 to have identified a previously unknown French son of Hitler.

RIGHT: *Stern* reporter Gerd Heidemann claimed that he had discovered Adolf Hitler's diaries, thus creating a hysterical media circus.

The literary fraud of the 1980s, and perhaps decades to come, was that of the Hitler diaries. The story broke on April 22, 1983, when Gerd Heidemann, a reporter for the West German magazine *Stern*, announced that he had recovered the secret diaries of Adolf Hitler. Since 1945, rumors about the existence and whereabouts of these long-lost documents had abounded. It was known that German officials had removed all of Hitler's papers and valuables from the Berlin bunker in which Nazi officials had taken refuge from the Russians.

Shortly before the end, Hitler had committed suicide, and the plane carrying his diaries went down in what would become East Germany. It was said that the journals had been handwritten by Hitler between 1932 and 1945. They comprised 62 magazine-size volumes bound in cheap leather covers and packed in a steel case. Supposedly, they had been retrieved from the wrecked plane by a German soldier or a nearby farmer and hidden in a hayloft for almost 40 years.

Before his public announcement, Heidemann had told his story to *Stern*, claiming he had been offered the diaries by a German dealer in Nazi artifacts whom he refused to name. Even so, the magazine's editors were so eager to obtain the diaries that they gave him almost $4 million to purchase them, and sold $3 million worth of serialization rights. Media tycoon Rupert Murdoch had allegedly paid $400,000 for British Commonwealth rights. *Life, Newsweek*, the *New York Post*, and the London *Sunday Times* were in for substantial sums.

After Heidemann's public announcement, in which he displayed several of the alleged diaries, euphoria ran high among media people and historians alike. Would the entire history of World War II have to be recast in light of this discovery? But within a few short weeks, skeptics spoke out clearly – both handwriting experts and historical authorities. Their objections were cogent.

The only survivors of the plane crash into East Germany had since died: there were no witnesses. It was known that Hitler's writing arm had been partially paralyzed in the 1944 assassination attempt by his own officers, but the journal entry for that July 20th made only a passing reference to the event. And even before the attempt on his life, Hitler wrote as little as possible because he was afflicted by Parkinson's Disease. Everything he "wrote," including *Mein Kampf*, had been dictated to a secretary. Further, among the countless documents that *had* been recovered from the Nazi regime, including the memoirs of Hitler's closest associates, there was no reference whatever to a diary.

New York autograph dealer Charles Hamilton made a close examination of the diaries and concluded that "I could have done better myself." He pointed out many discrepancies between the handwriting in Hitler's will and that of the journals. The letters were too carefully formed and too alike throughout the work, which was supposed to have covered a span of 13 years. Consultant Kenneth Rendell, whom *Newsweek* retained to authenticate the diaries before printing excerpts, was allowed to examine the first and last volumes. He discovered additional evidence of forgery.

In spite of the evidence, the London *Sunday Times* printed the first excerpt on April 25. Peter Koch, editor-in-chief of *Stern*, hotly defended the diaries, even flying to New York to display them on television. He claimed that the outcry against them was the result of jealousy on the part of other publishers. Of course, by this time he had a strong vested interest in their authenticity – not only the millions he had paid for them, but the reputation of his magazine, which was rapidly eroding.

Even as Koch traveled to New York, his editorial board voted to have the diaries examined by the nation's Federal Archives in Koblenz, headed by Hans Booms. On May 6, Booms held a news conference with West Germany's interior minister, Friedrich Zimmermann, who announced that "the Federal Archives is convinced the documents they were given were not produced by Hitler's hand, but were written in the post-war period." He went on to say that some of the entries had been plagiarized from a book by the former Nazi archivist Max Domarus: *Hitler's Speeches and Proclamations, 1932-45*.

With this announcement, Heidemann was arrested for fraud. He pointed to a confidence man named Konrad Kujau as the dealer who had sold him the documents. Kujau was arrested as he tried to cross the Bavarian border and the two were tried the following September. After a trial that dragged on for 11 months, both were convicted of fraud and sentenced to more than four years in prison.

Most of the $3 million they had been paid by *Stern* magazine was never recovered, and Peter Koch resigned as editor-in-chief. *Stern* made a public apology for the unprofessional way it had handled the story, but public confidence in the journal was shaken by the facts that came out at the trial. It had been a poorly conceived and executed deception, quickly unmasked – a nine days' wonder rather than the literary fraud of the century, but one that seriously undermined the credibility of several leading newspapers and magazines.

ABOVE: East German forger Konrad Kujau, whose own prolific hand produced an abundance of Hitler memorabilia, including the Hitler Diaries.

LEFT: In 1985 Kujau and Heidemann (pictured here during his trial) were each convicted of fraud and sentenced to more than four years' imprisonment.

CHAPTER FOUR

SWINDLING AS A FINE ART

Copying great works of art has a long history and need not involve deception. Art students have copied the work of their predecessors since the first paintings were made on the walls of caves. Roman artists copied the Greeks and in the process transmitted a vast cultural legacy to which they added the stamp of their own time, place, and values. But when an artist tries to pass off his own work as that of another, forgery and larceny come into the picture.

Even the world's great museums and art galleries have been deceived by skillful forgeries. In 1984 New York's Metropolitan Museum of Art announced that 45 of the masterworks in its collection – elegant gold pieces embellished with jewels in the manner of Benvenuto Cellini – were fraudulent. They had all been created by a German master craftsman named Reinhold Vasters during the nineteenth century.

The forgeries were revealed when a

PAGE 76: A fake entitled *Madonna and Child* by Alceo Dossena.

FAR LEFT: Artist and sculptor Amedeo Modigliani, the inspiration for an artist hoax of the 1980s.

BELOW: Benvenuto Cellini work was forged.

museum curator discovered the working drawings for a gold cup shaped like a sea-shell surmounting a dragon studded with jewels. In this case, technology played a part in the unveiling: the cup had been soldered together in a way unknown to the Renaissance. The piece was indeed a work of art – but not by Cellini. The Florentine goldsmith and sculptor was a Mannerist, whose best-known work is the gold saltcellar commissioned by Francis I of France early in the sixteenth century. This lavish piece, five years in the making, features the elongated figures of Earth and Neptune reclining on a boat-shaped bowl. Its base bears figures representing the four seasons and the four parts of the day. It is believed to be the artist's only surviving work in precious metal.

Another famous art hoax of the 1980s was revealed as the work of some enterprising art students in Livorno, Italy. The town was preparing to celebrate the 100th anniversary of the birth of native son Amedeo Modigliani. A pioneer of modern art, Modigliani was first a sculptor, only later a painter, as his health deteriorated and the physical labor of sculpting became too much for him. His paintings of women are recognizable for the mannered elongation of the subjects, and for their languid elegance.

Modigliani's sculptures, of which only 26 survive, have oval heads and stylized features of the same kind. Although the artist lived in Paris from 1906, and died in 1920 at the age of 35, it had been rumored for decades that long-lost sculptures by Modigliani were buried in the mud of Livorno's canal. It was said that the young artist had thrown them into the water in a fit of rage when friends criticized his work. In July 1984, the city's Progressive Museum of Contemporary Art undertook to dredge the canal in hope of finding the lost works for its centennial exhibition.

The first week of dredging produced nothing more exciting than some rusted bicycles and a rocking horse. But on July 24, excited townspeople and museum officials saw two stone sculptures retrieved from the depths. Two weeks later, a third was found. Art experts and publicists converged on Livorno. Then the news went out that the pieces were certainly the work of Modigliani. The museum cleaned them and put them into the exhibit, designated Modi 1, 2, and 3.

Not long afterward, three university students came forward to admit that they had carved the piece called Modi 2 as a prank after they heard about the dredging. They were surprised that their copy had fooled so many experts – their main idea had been to give the city fathers something to find. Shortly thereafter, a local laborer who had studied art presented himself as the creator of Modi 1 and 3. His objective was to show up the guillibility of the art critics and the media, who had been so quick to see what they wanted to.

In any case, Livorno did not lose out as a result of the fake Modiglianis. So many people came to see the exhibit that the museum made an unheard-of profit – far more than the cost of dredging the canal. The experts admitted sheepishly that they had been too hasty in their conclusions, and the art historians went right on speculating about the existence and whereabouts of the long-lost sculptures.

ABOVE: Three Italian university students (from left to right: Pietro Luridana, Francesco Ferrucci and Michele Ghelarducci) pose with the "Modigliani" sculpture they created as an innocent prank in Livorno during the 1980s.

FAR LEFT: An elaborately Renaissance covered cup – one of the exquisite artistic forgers created by Reinhold Vasters. Remarkably, New York's Metropolitan Museum of Art held over 40 of Vasters' works – credited to Benvenuto Cellini – in its collection. Their bogus nature was uncovered in the early 1980s.

Portraits of famous people have often been falsified, as in the case of Abraham Lincoln. In the absence of a full-length formal portrait of the president, lithographers set out to satisfy the public demand. Working from steel engravings of former statesmen like Henry Clay and John C. Calhoun, inventive artists transposed Lincoln's head on to their bodies. In some cases, the clothing was altered to that of the mid-nineteenth century. The Library of Congress has a whole collection of fake Lincoln portraits that have held honored places in American schoolrooms and town halls for a 100 years.

One of the best known is the oval lithograph depicting Lincoln with George Washington, entitled *The Father, and the Saviour of Our Country*. Another is the picture of Lincoln's head on the body of John C. Calhoun, in which the left hand rests on a copy of the Emancipation Proclamation, another late addition.

The more popular the artist, the likelier it is that spurious works will bear his or her signature. Anthony Van Dyck, the seventeenth-century Flemish artist, painted some 70 pictures in his lifetime, most of them refined portraits of the English aristocracy. A gifted apprentice of Peter Paul Rubens, Van Dyck became court painter to Charles I of England in 1632. His fluid Baroque portraits, including *Charles I Hunting*, were extremely influential in England and on the Continent. At this writing, almost 2000

ABOVE: Can you spot the fake? A curator posed with two versions of Spanish master Diego Velasquez's portrait of Cardinal Borgia. The lefthand picture had been in the Frankfurt, Germany, gallery for over 70 years; the righthand painting was obtained from a local private source.

RIGHT: A painting attributed to the Spanish artist Goya entitled *The Marquesa de Santa Cruz as the Muse Euterpe*. It was to be auctioned as genuine — with an estimate price of $12 million — until the Spanish government questioned its authenticity.

FAR RIGHT: A member of the French police's forgery section examines two fakes, one masquerading as a Van Gogh (top) and the other as a Picasso.

paintings, many in the world's museums and art collections, have been attributed to him.

The French classical landscape painter Jean-Baptiste Camille Corot produced some 3000 pictures during his career.

During the nineteenth century, he traveled widely to sketch from nature, then transferred these scenes to large canvases in his studio. Today, the spontaneous sketches are considered his finest work, but during his lifetime such large-scale paintings as *La Rochelle*, done in misty pastel colors, were in great demand. It has been estimated that more than 8000 fake Corots have been foisted off on inexperienced buyers. The number of forged Picassos, Dalis, and Van Goghs must be incalculably higher.

Sometimes an honest artist is duped by his agents, as in the case of Alceo Dossena, whose reproductions of antique sculptures were never intended to deceive. In *Hoaxes That Made Headlines*, Silverstein and Arnold tell the story of this gifted Italian stonecutter turned sculptor. Apprenticed to a marble mason near Cremona at the turn of the century, he had been drawing since childhood and showed great aptitude for carving. The mason taught him how to repair antique sculptures, monuments, and columns and to carve replacement pieces in the manner of Michelangelo and other masters of the Renaissance. These pieces were then aged by various techniques until it was very hard to tell that they were skillful reproductions.

In 1916 Dossena sold one of his antique madonnas to a local jeweler named Alberto Fasoli – a clever confidence man. Fasoli realized that he could get rich selling Dossena's carvings as original works of art. He formed a partnership with a dishonest antique dealer named Romano Palesi, and they set up a studio in Rome for the young sculptor. There Dossena spent almost 10 years working for a small monthly salary, while his agents made several million dollars selling his pieces as originals.

Over the years, Dossena branched out into new styles and media. He made wooden altarpieces in the Gothic mode, classical Greek sculptures aged in acid baths, and figures in clay and bronze. Fasoli and Palesi sold them to collectors, art dealers, and museums around the world. The scheme fell apart only after Dossena went to Fasoli for money after his wife died in 1927, leaving him deeply in debt. (He had made only $30,000 over the decade of his relationship with the dishonest agents.) When Fasoli turned him away, Dossena filed a lawsuit, and the ensuing publicity alerted purchasers of his work to the deception.

Unfortunately, Dossena himself was the fraud's major victim. He continued to work for another 10 years but had little success in selling his pieces and died in poverty in 1937.

Two other art frauds of recent times involved sustained and ingenious deception.

PAGES 86-87: Early French Impressionist Jean-Baptiste Camille Corot has been a popular subject with art forgers. As an artist with a huge body of work, estimated at over 3000 paintings, it is easier to pass off bogus images as his. This *Landscape with Two Peasant Ladies* in the style of Corot is a fake.

LEFT: Bogus paintings in the style of Rembrandt, Dali, Picasso and Goya, among others, adorn a room in the home of German Konrad Kujau. Kujau was later to gain international fame as one of the driving forces behind the so-called Hitler Diaries.

The first is the case of Hans van Meegeren, a Dutch artist who was imprisoned as a Nazi collaborator because of his talent for painting like Vermeer van Delft. The seventeenth-century Dutch master painted brilliant studies in light and shade, which took so much time that he produced only 40 known paintings in his lifetime.

During World War II, the Nazis confiscated many valuable works of art from conquered countries, including a Vermeer entitled *The Adultress*, which was purchased by Air Marshal Hermann Goering. After the war, the Allied Art Commission was formed to restore such national treasures to their respective owners. When the painting was traced to a Dutch artist named van Meegeren, the authorities arrested him as a collaborator with the Nazis because he refused to reveal how he had come to own it. During his trial, the whole incredible story of the forgeries came out.

As a child in Deventer, van Meegeren had shown great talent for drawing, which was encouraged by his parents and teachers. In high school, he was deeply influenced by the Dutch masters Rembrandt, Vermeer, and Frans Hals, whose works he copied assiduously. Guided by his art teacher, he learned how to grind pigments and make paints as they had done.

In 1913 he won an award for one of his watercolors at The Hague and was accepted as an art student there. After taking his degree, he enjoyed some success in selling his work, but by 1930, his career was in a decline. His bitterness increased when a local art critic offered to review his work favorably for a bribe.

Van Meegeren turned to forgery as much for revenge on the artistic establishment as for money. His ambition was to create a Vermeer that would fool such experts and be acquired by a major museum.

FAR LEFT: Hans van Meegeren faces his accusers. Van Meegeren was a great admirer of Vermeer to the extent he successfully forged many of the Old Master's works.

BELOW: Van Meegeren's *Last Supper at Emmaus* posing as an original Vermeer. In 1947 the forger was tried and convicted on fraud charges. Three months later he was dead.

Van Meegeren was well aware of the things that would betray him to the experts, such as the use of modern canvas and pigments. He bought inexpensive seventeenth-century paintings and removed all the paint, then compounded his paints just as Vermeer had done. He aged his work by baking the canvases, introducing hairline cracks, and brushing the compositions with India ink, which he wiped off for an antique effect. He spent four years perfecting his techniques, then began work on the painting he called *Last Supper at Emmaus*.

Like most Vermeers, it was a strong, simple composition; Christ and his disciples were seated at a table near a window through which light poured in upon the scene, which takes place after the Resurrection. When van Meegeren had completed the painting, he tore the edges of the canvas to make it look frayed, then sent it to Dr. Bredius for authentication.

The elderly art critic was enthralled by the work. He wrote a certificate of authentication describing van Meegeren's painting as "This glorious work of Vermeer, the great Vermeer of Delft." Art magazines picked up the story and Holland's Boyman's Museum ultimately bought the painting for some $250,000.

Originally, it had been van Meegeren's plan to announce how he had duped the experts once the painting was sold. But the great amount of money involved changed his mind: instead, he would become rich from the sale of his "Old Masters." During the next two years, he painted a scene he called *Interior with Drinkers* in the style of Pieter de Hooch and another fake Vermeer, *The Last Supper*. Both were purchased by a wealthy collector. Five more Vermeers followed in rapid succession, one of which was purchased by Amsterdam's renowned Rijksmuseum.

During the war years, van Meegeren slid rapidly into drug and alcohol addiction. His postwar arrest as a Nazi collaborator was a blow from which he never recovered. After six weeks in prison, he admitted that *The Adultress* was not a Vermeer at all: he had painted it himself. At first, no one believed him. He then confessed that he had painted other Vermeers, including those in the national museums. Finally, the authorities agreed to provide him with a studio and materials so that he could prove his claim. Under the watchful eye of two policemen, he painted a new masterwork in the manner of Vermeer: *The Young Christ Teaching in the Temple*.

FAR LEFT: Nazi Air Marshal Hermann Goering was an avid collector and looter of art. His and van Meegeren's paths crossed when the Marshal purchased the Dutch hoaxer's "Vermeer" *The Adultress*.

BELOW: U.S. troops gather up some of the paintings plundered by leading Nazis during World War II.

FAR RIGHT: *The Artist as Rembrandt with Titus*, one of the works created by English artist Tom Keating. Keating became something of a television personality for his openness. He claimed that he was not passing off his work as Old Masters for money but simply to get his paintings noticed.

BELOW: David Stein, also known as Georges Delauney and Michel Honcourt, returns to the limelight some while after a jail term for forging the works of many masters of modern art. He was later recognized as an accomplished artist in his own right.

The public was intrigued by media coverage of the event, and several art critics looked very foolish, but van Meegeren's troubles were not over. In 1947 he was tried for fraud and convicted. His health broke down completely, and within three months he was dead. Only after his death was the real merit of his own youthful work more fully recognized.

In many ways, it is much easier to produce fraudulent works of modern art, especially in light of the sophisticated scientific techniques now available for detecting artistic chicanery. Antique paintings are harder to fake. Neutron autoradiography makes it possible to isolate the chemical composition of various materials used in paintings alleged to be centuries old. Through this process, New York's Pierpont Morgan Library discovered that one of its "medieval" manuscripts contained copper arsenite – a material not in use until the late 1700s.

Routine chemical analysis of oil paint samples can prove that a work is much newer than it is purported to be. Other devices for debunking works of art include infrared photography, reflectography, and S-rays, which reveal sketches and paintings covered by overpainting the same canvas. Pigments can also be heated to high temperatures, at which experts can measure the light they emit to determine the age of an artwork.

The forger of modern art can use contemporary canvas, paper, and materials with impunity. One artist who has made a lucrative career of modern-art forgeries is known variously as David Stein, Georges Delauney, and Michel Honcourt. He made a fortune during the 1960s producing fake Picassos, Modiglianis, and Chagalls. However, the risks attendant upon imitating artists who are still alive finally caught up with him. Some of his "Chagall" drawings were shown to Marc Chagall by a suspicious New York art dealer, and the artist declared them to be fraudulent. Eventually, Stein was sentenced to three years in prison on 97 counts of forgery. He spent his time there painting and sold 50 canvases to a London dealer at a handsome price. It is one of life's many mysteries that the artistic confidence man is so often exceptionally gifted and well able to produce enduring work that bears his own signature.

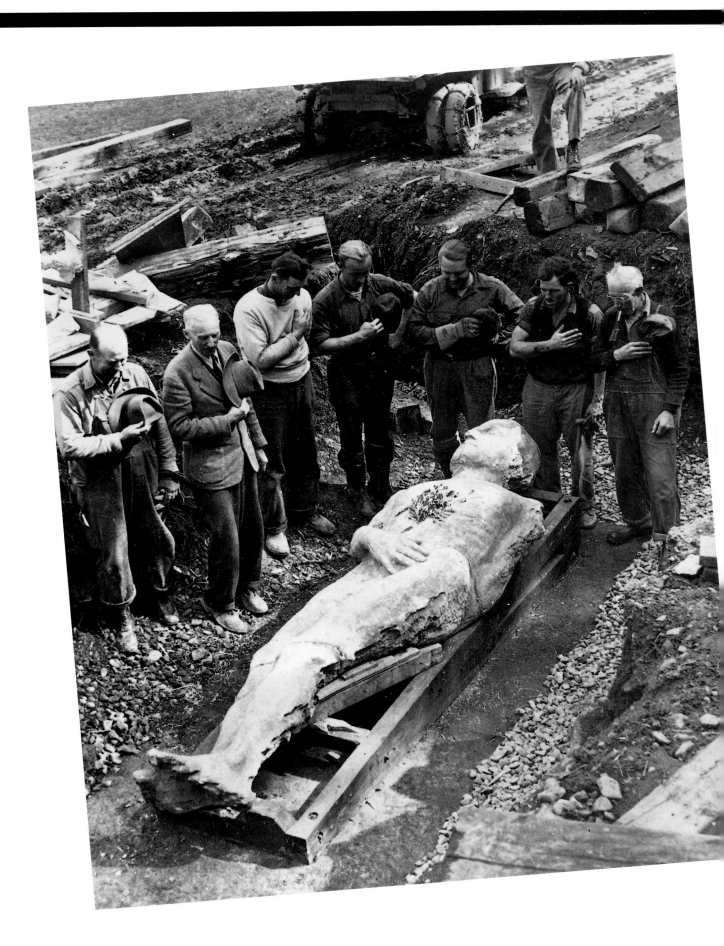

CHAPTER FIVE

PSEUDO-SCIENCE

The Industrial Revolution, modern technology, psychoanalysis, and archaeology have all played a part in the enduring fascination with science over the last 200 years. However, most people only know enough about it to be easily fooled by con men and hoaxers who present themselves as experts on the subject. In the early 1860s, Mark Twain had fun with readers of the Virginia City *Territorial Enterprise*, where he was a young reporter, with his story of the Petrified Man.

At the time, amateur archaeologists were roaming the Nevada hills to dig up what Twain called "petrifactions." His satire on this craze for collecting fossils, arrowheads, and other relics reported that the seated figure of a man turned to stone had been discovered embedded in a nearby cliff. A curious feature of it was that one leg had been replaced by a wooden leg. When an inquest was held, the coroner determined that the petrified man had died of protracted exposure.

Local citizens thought it a good joke, but other newspapers across the country picked up the story and printed it as sober fact. The temptation to embellish the tale was irresistible, so Twain produced a sequel. Supposedly, an assayer had analyzed some soil from the petrified man's big toenail and announced that he had originated in "the Kingdom of New Jersey." Moreover, the fossil remains would be exhibited in a glass case at the local library in the interest of science.

No one knows how many credulous readers visited the library to view the Petrified Man from New Jersey, but after several more hoaxes of this type, Twain's paper put him on notice that *Enterprise* reporters were not paid to write fiction. Soon afterward, Twain migrated to California to write wild stories for the *San Francisco Call*.

In 1835 *New York Sun* reporter Richard Adams Locke increased circulation from 2500 to 19,000 by reporting that the renowned British astronomer Sir John Herschel had built a giant telescope in South Africa and discovered life on the Moon. According to Locke, Herschel had observed great bison-like creatures with hairy flaps over their eyes to protect them from extreme light; goat-sized blue monsters with

PAGE 96: Reburying a papier mâché replica of the "Cardiff Giant," a 3000-pound stone figure found on a farm in Cardiff, New York, in 1869. Although the original, the brainchild of con artist and cigar maker George Hull, was quickly revealed as a fake by scientists, the figure, believed by many to be the remains of a member of a race of giants from the prehistoric era, attracted the paying public in droves. Hull made a quick fortune.

FAR LEFT: Mark Twain, first and foremost renowned as a writer of novels, was also a great hoaxer. As a journalist, he took great delight in feeding the reading public believable but utterly bogus stories.

LEFT: Eminent British astronomer Sir John Herschel was the unwitting participant in a hoax news story perpetrated by journalist Richard Adams Locke. In 1835 Locke claimed that Herschel, working in South Africa, had discovered the existence of "Moon People" by the use of a sophisticated telescope. Members of the public were convinced; Herschel, when he read the story, was amused; Locke made $25,000 selling pamphlets which illustrated the strange beings.

beards and a single horn; and "a strange amphibious creature of a spherical form, which rolled with great velocity across the pebbly beach." This weird assortment of fauna inhabited pyramid-shaped mountains of amethyst near a lake 260 miles long.

Interest was immediate and intense. Locke's articles concluded with an illustrated description of the "Moon People," who stood about four feet high, had wings from shoulder to calf at rest, and were covered with copper-colored hair except on their faces. The stories were full of scientific terminology and impressed both the press and the public.

The *New York Times* said that they displayed "the most extensive and accurate knowledge of astronomy," and a group of Springfield, Massachusetts, women began raising funds to send missionaries to the Moon. Finally, the stories reached Sir John Herschel, who laughingly disclaimed them, and the Moon People were left to their own devices. Bound up in pamphlet form, the articles had already sold 60,000 copies for $25,000, so Locke could well afford to lose his job at the *Sun*.

Another nineteenth-century exercise in pseudo-science was the case of the Cardiff Giant, a 3000-pound stone-figure "found" on a farm in Cardiff, New York, in 1869. For weeks, visitors crowded Stub Newell's

property to peer down into the pit where the giant had been unearthed. He was a stocky figure with huge limbs and rugged features, stained by centuries of lying beneath the earth. The find gave credence to ancient tales of a race of giants, and Newell erected a tent over the pit and charged 50 cents admission. On a single Sunday, 2500 people came to stare and be amazed.

Scientists like Yale University's O. C. Marsh promptly denounced the giant as a fake, but the public was undeterred. Many were convinced that the giant was a petrified man from the prehistoric period, while others believed him to be an ancient statue. Meanwhile, the sleepy town of Cardiff, population 200, was booming, as tourists came by rail and wagon to patronize the local merchants and stay at the two hotels. Impromptu cider stands sprang up in front of houses and several restaurants opened.

The object of all this excitement was the creation of a Binghamton, New York, con man and cigar maker named George Hull. He got the idea of making a stone giant when he visited Iowa in 1866 and talked with a traveling preacher about the giants mentioned in the Book of Genesis. On a return trip to Iowa, he visited the gypsum quarries near Fort Dodge with his partner, H. B. Martin. They hired a stonecutter to quarry a block 12 feet high by four feet wide,

FAR LEFT: A reproduction of Sir John Herschel's 20-inch telescope through which it was claimed that the astronomer had identified creatures on the Moon by American journalist Richard Locke.

BELOW: An extremely fanciful artistic impression of the "Moon People" and various other lunar animals. The creatures, seen here in flight, were described as being four feet in height, having wings attached to their bodies from shoulder to calf, and being covered in copper-colored hair.

LEFT: The ''Cardiff Giant'' towers over Stub Newell, the farmer on whose land the hoax was uncovered. Newell was, in fact, cousin to the con perpetrator George Hull.

THE GREAT

CARDIFF GIANT!

Discovered at Cardiff, Onondaga Co., N. Y., is now on Exhibition in the

Geological Hall, Albany,

For a few days only.

HIS DIMENSIONS.

Length of Body, - - 10 feet, 4 1-2 inches.
Length of Head from Chin to Top of Head, 21 ''
Length of Nose, - - - - 6 ''
Across the Nostrils, - - - 3 1-2 ''
Width of Mouth, - - - 5 ''
Circumference of Neck, - - - 37 ''
Shoulders, from point to point, 3 feet, 1 1-2 ''
Length of Right Arm, - 4 feet, 9 1-2 ''
Across the Wrist, - - - 5 ''
Across the Palm of Hand, - - - 7 ''
Length of Second Finger, - - 8 ''
Around the Thighs, - 6 feet, 3 1-2 ''
Diameter of the Thigh, - - 13 ''
Through the Calf of Leg, - - 9 1-2 ''
Length of Foot, - - - 21 ''
Across the Ball of Foot, - - 8 ''
Weight, - - - - 2990 pounds.

ALBANY, November 29th, 1869.

ABOVE: The dimension of the ''Cardiff Giant'' displaced on an advertisement. The figure was in fact carved out of gypsum and artificially aged with wet sand, ink and sulphuric acid, and was then buried for a year before it was ''unexpectedly'' discovered.

ABOVE, FAR RIGHT: The moment when the gypsum giant was removed from its ''grave'' on Newell's Onandaga County, New York, farm in 1869.

FAR RIGHT: John W. Keely photographed in his laboratory. In 1872, Keely announced to the world that he had invented a powerful engine that ran on water. Surprisingly, investors leapt at the chance to invest in his wholly impractical machine.

then shipped the stone to Chicago. There a pair of sculptors spent three months carving it into the shape of a man and aging it with wet sand, ink, and sulphuric acid.

When the figure was complete, Hull shipped it to his cousin Stub Newell, who buried it on his farm. The conspirators waited a year before discovering the Cardiff giant under five feet of topsoil and unveiling him to an eager public.

Hull knew that the statue would soon be discredited by experts, so while the sensation was at its height, he sold his interest to local businessmen for $30,000. They soon moved the giant to Syracuse, where the crowds – and the take – were even bigger. Strangely enough, interest was unabated even after paleontologists proved that gypsum was not a local stone and that the Cardiff Giant was a fraud. P. T. Barnum made a replica of it for exhibition and the original giant ended up in the Farmer's Museum at Cooperstown, New York, where it remains to this day.

Rube Goldberg-type inventions had a heyday during the nineteenth century, when man's fascination with machinery could be profitably combined with the promise of health and wealth. In 1894 a Philadelphia engineer named W. C. Crosley invented a machine that turned flour paste into ''coffee beans'' that could be dyed brown and mixed with the real thing to increase the manufacturer's profits. Crosley made about half a million dollars from this and other devices, including a fake ice-making machine and "talking" motion pictures whose syncopated sound came from hidden phonograph records.

Prescott Jernegan, a former Baptist missionary, came up with the lucrative "Gold Accumulator" in 1897. Painted with mercury and "a secret chemical," it was immersed in sea water to attract loose gold floating in the currents. Its powers were "proved" when Jernegan's partner, a skillful diver, swam out to the closely guarded device and replaced the original accumulator with a gold-encrusted one. Connecticut investors lost about $350,000 before the perpetrators took off for Europe to live in high style.

The energy-machine scam was tried often and successfully on a believing public. In 1872 John Keely demonstrated a machine that he claimed could power a 30-car train from New York to Philadelphia on a quart of water. "With these three agents alone – air, water, and machine," he proclaimed, "I once drove an engine 800 revolutions per

minute of 40 horse power with less than a thimbleful of water and kept it running 15 days." Investors lined up to buy stock.

Some 50 years later, Walter Hohenau (who declaimed modestly, "I am but a scientist") convinced thousands that his machine could produce hydrogen gas from atoms. Others came up with inventions guaranteed to turn water into gasoline.

During the early days of radio, a Chicago con man convinced listeners that deadly "radio waves" were emanating from their sets. The pernicious effects could be overcome only by exposure to his "Radio Opposer," which beamed "benevolent rays" on to the afflicted person for a hefty cash payment. The treatment had to be renewed periodically, and it included a dose of "radio pills" – baking soda compressed into tablets.

In 1912 an unknown person, perhaps an archaeology student, touched off 40 years of controversy among scientists around the world when he fabricated a human fossil. It was discovered in a gravel pit near Piltdown Common, in the county of Sussex, England, by a respected amateur archaeologist named Charles Dawson. A local workman had showed him a fossilized bone he had found in the pit, and Dawson started digging. Soon he turned up the fossilized skull and jawbone of an ape-like man that appeared to be half a million years old. The skull bone was extremely thick and the forehead steep, unlike the low, sloping forehead of the Neanderthal Man previously discovered in Germany. The mandible and jaw resembled those of a chimpanzee, but contained two human teeth. Could this be the Missing Link in Darwin's renowned theory of evolution?

As Dawson explored the gravel pit for additional fossils, he was joined by two respected men of science: Dr. Arthur Smith Woodward, head of the Geology Department at the British Museum, and Pierre Teil-

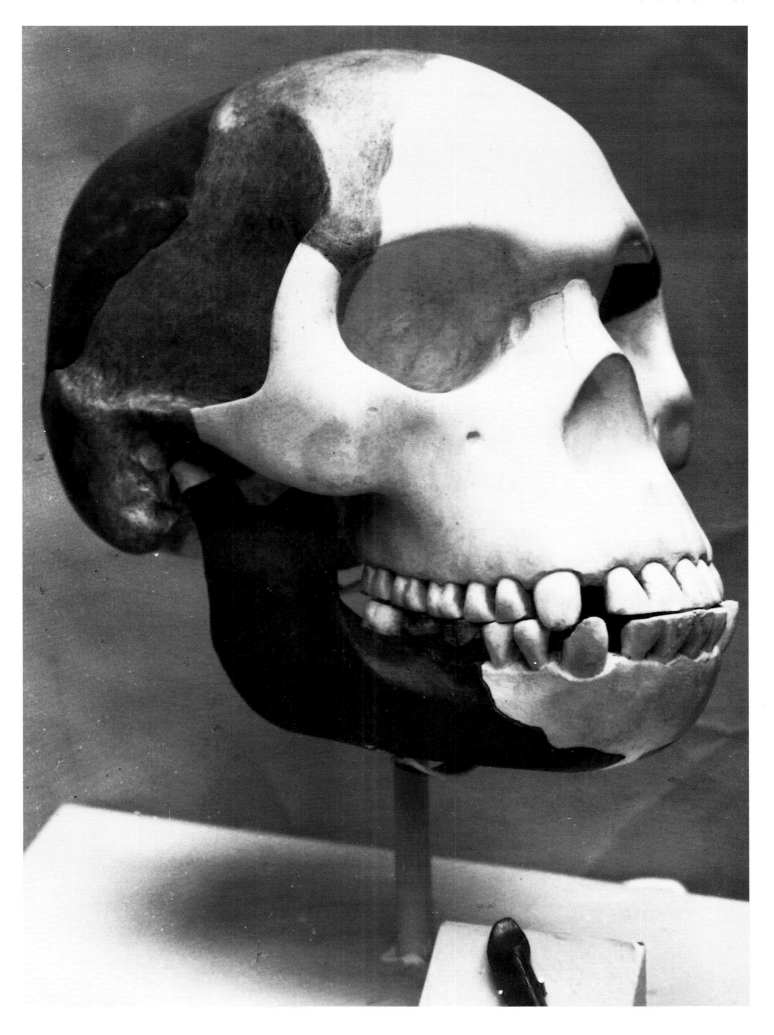

hard de Chardin, a novice in the Society of Jesus and a French paleontologist of growing renown. The British magazine *Nature* wrote up the discovery as one of major importance, concluding: "Dr. Smith Woodward ... inclines to the theory that the Neanderthal race was a degenerate offshoot of early Man, while surviving modern Man may have arisen directly from a primitive source of which the Piltdown skull provides the first discovered evidence." When Dr. Smith Woodward wrote a book about Piltdown man, he called it *The Earliest Englishman*, which gave the discovery an aura of national pride.

American scholars from the Museum of Natural History in New York City were more cautious in their enthusiasm. They were troubled by the fact that the jawbone did not seem to match the skull; it was too much like that of a chimpanzee. The museum exhibited a replica of the Piltdown discovery in a glass case, but made no extravagant

BELOW: French paleontologist and Jesuit priest Pierre Teilhard de Chardin was one of the first to excavate the Piltdown Common gravel pits in the search for further remains of the faked skull. No one has even been able to uncover the individual or individuals who set up this most renowned of scientific con tricks.

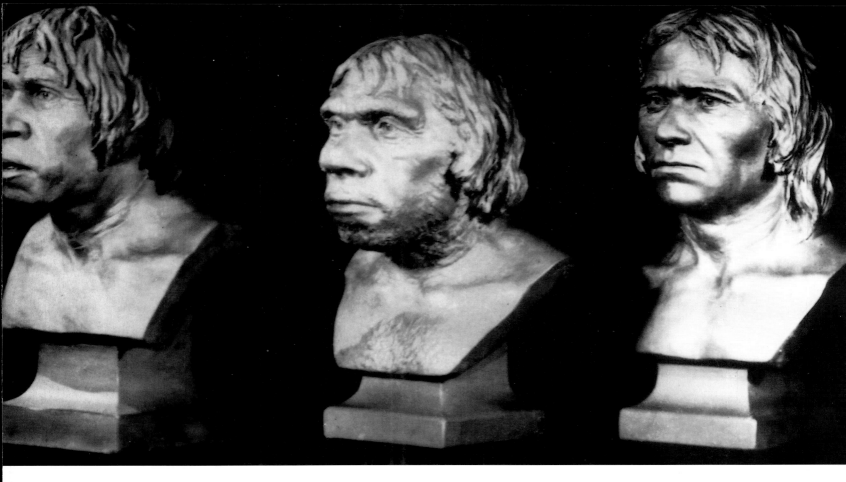

claims on the identification card, which read in part, "The brain case represents a very early and human type."

The initial excitement was reawakened when Dawson found several pieces of skull and another tooth two miles from the Piltdown site in 1915. It seemed impossible that the two finds could be coincidental. When Dawson died in his late forties the following year, a memorial stone was erected to him at the Piltdown site. But as the years went by, other discoveries in England and abroad added to the understanding of human evolution without shedding any light on Piltdown Man, who didn't seem to fit in anywhere. At this point, no one suspected fraud, but a leading British paleontologist spoke of Piltdown Man as "the Piltdown enigma."

The 1930s brought major fossil finds which showed that the human jaw and teeth started evolving toward their present form earlier than the skull. How, then, to account for the modern forehead and ape-like jaw of the Piltdown remains? Some anthropologists theorized that man had descended from the apes in two separate lines, one of which was represented by Piltdown Man. But why had no other specimens of this type been discovered?

The answer came only gradually, with new means of dating fossil remains. The first was the fluorine test, designed to measure the age of a fossil by the fluorine content acquired over long periods in the earth. Dr. Kenneth Page Oakley of the British Museum applied this test to the Pilt-down remains in 1949 and reported to the British Geological Society that they were much less than half a million years old. Subsequently, dental analysis of the teeth revealed that they were modern – the appearance of age and wear had been achieved by grinding them down artificially.

In 1953 a congress of paleontologists met in London and decided to apply still more rigorous tests to the Piltdown remains. Those involved included Dr. Oakley, Dr. J. S. Weiner of Oxford University, and University of Chicago scholar S. L. Washburn. After subjecting the Piltdown remains to additional fluorine tests, X-rays, and extensive chemical analyses, they made the joint announcement that Piltdown Man was a fake. The skull was modern, artificially aged, and the jaw was that of a monkey. As the dental researcher had previous asserted, the teeth were human.

The scientific world, and the public, were shocked. But as the announcement sank in, there was relief, as well: now the pattern emerging from other fossil discoveries became coherent. As Sir Mortimer Wheeler put it: "The new Piltdown discovery removed an awkward customer from the line of human evolution."

There was much speculation about the identity of the hoaxer, perhaps long dead, who had planted the skull and jawbone in the gravel pit at Piltdown some 40 years before. Dr. Weiner wrote a book entitled *The Piltdown Forgeries* which suggested that Dawson himself had faked the discovery to enhance his reputation as an archaeologist.

ABOVE: The evolution of the skull of early man, showing the supposed position of "Piltdown Man" in the scheme of things. This imposter is second from left.

But others closely concerned, including Teilhard de Chardin, denied categorically that Dawson could have been the culprit. The answer may never be known.

Another archaeological find that turned out to be fraudulent was that made by a San Francisco picnicker in 1936. It was a weathered brass plaque that bore an inscription signed by Sir Francis Drake, the first Englishman to circumnavigate the globe, beginning in 1577. The ship's journal for the voyage shows that Drake rounded the tip of South America and sailed up the west coast of both the Americas, making a landfall in 1579 somewhere near what is now San Francisco. He claimed the region for England, calling it New Albion, and left a brass plaque at the site.

At first, the picnicker paid little attention to his find, but several months later he washed it off and found an illegible inscription. He turned the plaque over to Dr. Herbert E. Bolton, director of the Bancroft Library in Berkeley, and the professor deciphered the inscription, which appeared to be Drake's claim to northern California in the name of Queen Elizabeth I. Tests of the metal at Columbia University in New York City indicated that the plaque was quite old, and it was installed at the Bancroft Library as an exhibit.

However, both British and American scholars found fault with the language of the inscription; the spellings were not consistent with those of Elizabethan English, and some of the phrasing was too modern. Harvard University's naval historian, the

highly regarded Samuel Eliot Morison, was not convinced either. He said that the plate was a forgery.

In 1978, two years before the 400th anniversary of Drake's landing, a new investigation of the plate was undertaken and proved that it was, indeed, a fake. Modern metal tests showed that the brass had been rolled – a method unknown in the sixteenth century – and that the edges had been cut rather than chiseled. However, the Bancroft Library kept the relic on display, along with the account of how its inauthenticity was discovered. Like the discredited Cardiff Giant, Sir Francis Drake's brass plaque remained an object of curiosity, often visited by the public and scholars alike.

College students are famous for their pseudo-scientific jokes on their professors, and Norman Moss tells of a legendary case in *The Pleasures of Deception*. It happened generations ago and is still remembered at his alma mater; Hamilton College in upstate New York:

"It seems that some students one year took the body of a spider, the wings of a dragon fly, the head of something else and the tail of something else, and glued them together. They took the resulting specimen to a biology professor as a strange bug they had found, and asked whether he could identify it. The professor looked at it closely and said, 'Hmmm, this is very interesting. Was it humming when you saw it?'

'Yes, it was,' they replied.

'In that case,' he said, 'I think it must be a hum bug.'"

FRANCISCVS DRAECK NOBILISSIMVS EQVES ANGLIÆ AN° ÆT SVE 43

CHAPTER SIX

FAMOUS IMPOSTORS

fig: 14

The Kings Balcon

A Floating Village

fig: 15

A Gentlemans Balcon

A Litter

One of history's most successful impostors was George Psalmanazar (not his real name, which is still unknown). He arrived in England in 1702 calling himself the "Native of Formosa" and claiming that he had been converted to Christianity by English missionaries. During this great age of exploration, people were always eager to hear tales of far-off, exotic lands, and Psalmanazar's imposture was successful from the first. He was lionized by society and offered a grant to study at Christ Church College, Oxford, so that he could train missionaries himself.

At Oxford, Psalmanazar wrote a book filled with outrageous stories that were swallowed whole by his admirers. He said that the Formosan religion was more blood-thirsty than that of the Aztecs: 18,000 boys a year were offered as human sacrifices. Polygamy was widely practiced; most of his countrymen lived to the age of 100; and the island was inhabited by elephants, giraffes and rhinoceri. His book fell into the hands of a Dutch Jesuit who had actually been to Formosa and who objected to Psalmanazar's account, but the author promptly denounced his critic and the public preferred his fantasies to the sober truth.

Psalmanazar spent 25 comfortable years as the Native of Formosa, handsomely supported and much sought after as an expert on the mysterious East. As so often happens, when he decided to reveal his imposture (the result of a religious conversion) most people didn't believe him, or didn't care. He remained good friends with Samuel Johnson and other intellectuals of the day, who always enjoyed his witty conversation and wide-ranging knowledge. But no one ever learned who he really was.

After the French Revolution died down, innumerable claimants to the title of Louis XVII, son and heir of France's last Bourbon king, stepped forward to assert their royalty. These "Lost Dauphins," as they were called, claimed to have been smuggled out of the French prison where the true prince had allegedly died of scurvy in 1795 at the age of 11.

One such pretender was Henri Herbert, an Austrian who appeared in France in 1818 to claim that he had been rescued from the prison cell by hiding in a toy horse in which another child had been brought in to take

The Formolan Alphabet

Name	Power			Figure				Name
Am	A	a	ao					
Mem	M	m̄	m					
Nen	N	n̄	n					
Taph	T	th	t					
Lamdo	L	ll	l					
Samdo	S	ch	s					
Vomera	V	w	u					
Bagdo	B	b	b					
Hamno	H	kh	h					
Pedlo	P	pp	p					
Kaphi	K	k	ж					
Omda	O	o	ω					
Itda	I	y	i					
Xatara	X	xh	x					
Dam	D	th	d					
Zamphi	Z	tf	z					
Epsi	E	ε	η					
Fandem	F	ph	f					
Raw	R	rh	r					
Gomera	G	g	j					

his place. His tale grew even more fantastic when he described the years after his rescue, including a long stay with a tribe of ''Mamelucks.'' Eventually, Herbert was tried for imposture and sentenced to 12 years in prison.

Another improbable claimant to the French throne was an American missionary named Eleazar Williams, who had served in the War of 1812. He said he had been raised by Indians in New York State after being rescued from prison as a child and smuggled across the Atlantic. Moreover the Prince of Joinville – next in line for the throne – had visited the United States and, during the journey, had him sign abdication papers in return for a lifelong pension from the French government.

When he changed his mind and tried to assert his identity as Louis XVII, the prince denied the whole story. William's claims were pooh-poohed in France, but a number of fellow Americans believed him. In fact, the Daughters of the American Revolution

erected a monument to him near his home in Green Bay, Wisconsin, and the Wisconsin Conservation Department dedicated Lost Dauphin State Park to his memory. The legend of the Lost Dauphin was so popular that Mark Twain drew on it for the comic character of the Dauphin in his *Adventures of Huckleberry Finn*. Not surprisingly, the Dauphin and his partner were both consummate con artists.

A case that became a byword for length and complexity was that of the Tichborne claimant, Arthur Orton, who announced himself to Victorian England as the long-lost heir to large estates and a baronetcy in Hampshire. The real Roger Tichborne had been lost at sea off South America after leaving England in 1852. His Roman Catholic family had objected to his engagement to his first cousin, Katherine Doughty, as a marriage between cousins so closely related is forbidden by the Church.

However, Katherine's father promised to seek a dispensation for the marriage if Roger

would leave his cousin for three years. The lovers exchanged vows, and Roger wrote a letter which he showed to Katherine before he left. She copied it, and he entrusted it to a friend. It stated that he would build a chapel at Tichborne to the Blessed Virgin if their hopes of marriage were fulfilled.

When Roger's ship, the *Bella*, went down in a storm off Rio de Janeiro, the courts waited three years before pronouncing him dead. His younger brother Alfred inherited the title, but died at the age of 27, leaving an infant son as the future baronet.

The unfortunate Dowager Lady Tichborne, who had lost her three other children, refused to believe that Roger was dead. She began advertising for news of him in colonial newspapers, one of which found its way to a bureau of missing persons in Australia. A lawyer's office posted the notice, and it was seen by a butcher who called himself Thomas Castro, living in the town of Wagga Wagga.

He informed the lawyer that he was Roger Tichborne and initiated a correspondence with Lady Tichborne, who wanted desperately to believe that his claim was true. She sent him to an old family servant named Bogle, then living in Sydney, and Castro convinced the man that he was the missing Roger. On funds supplied by Lady Tichborne, he sailed for England with the elderly servant, and his own wife and two children.

Lady Tichborne settled an allowance of 1000 pounds a year on Castro, and he took up residence in Hampshire to cultivate an acquaintance with Roger's friends and neighbors. Apparently, the only two people who disbelieved his claim were Roger's old tutor and his friend Vincent Gosport, to whom he had entrusted his letter to Katherine. When Castro claimed that he couldn't

remember what was in the letter, Gosport was sure he was an impostor. Nevertheless, Castro went to the Chancery Division of the Court, in charge of wills and estates, and asserted that he was Sir Roger Tichborne, which would invalidate the claim of his brother Alfred's son Henry. Attorneys for the child's family entered the fray. It was to become the longest criminal trial in British history to that date.

While the case was still in Chancery, Castro perjured himself and slandered Katherine Doughty, now married to a man named Joseph Radcliffe, by saying that she had told him she was pregnant to force him into marriage. Vincent Gosport had destroyed Roger's letter upon learning of his death, so it could not be produced in evidence against Castro's claim. Not only the

families involved, but the public, took sides with passionate vehemence. A man named J. B. Atley said of Castro's slur on Katherine that "A blacker lie was never committed to paper." Many agreed with him. Others were equally convinced that the Tichborne claimant was acting in a just cause and even contributed to his legal expenses.

Early in 1871, the court heard some 90 witnesses testify that Castro was the Roger Tichborne they had known. Among them were members of the Sixth Dragoons, Roger's former regiment, and a governess in the Tichborne family. Then Castro himself took the stand, creating a bad impression by his ignorance about Roger's boyhood and the subjects he had studied in school. Another damaging bit of testimony came from the Tichborne family lawyers, who identified the claimant with a man named Arthur Orton, who had left his family in Wapping to emigrate to Australia years before. There he had vanished after being accused of horse theft.

Castro's claim eroded still further when Katherine Doughty Radcliffe testified movingly about the missing letter and Roger's promise to build a chapel if they should marry. Lady Tichborne had died before the case came to trial, but two of her sisters swore that Castro was not their nephew, Roger. Finally, several witnesses produced the most damning evidence of all: Roger Tichborne's initials had been tattooed on his forearm.

Once the civil jury gave its verdict that the claimant was not Roger Tichborne, the Lord Chief Justice ordered him arrested for perjury. But his supporters soon had him freed on bail, and he canvassed the country drumming up sympathy – and funds – for his defense. He appeared at music halls, lawn fetes, and public meetings, generating a surprising amount of support. All of England was either for or against "the claimant," as he was called.

When the criminal case came to trial a year later, Castro was represented by an over-zealous Irish lawyer named Edward Kenealy who spent 23 days summing up the case; the trial dragged on for 188 days. There was little doubt of the outcome after the claimant introduced perjured evidence about his rescue from the sinking *Bella*. (The sailor who swore that they were in the same lifeboat proved to have been in jail at the time.) The Tichborne family produced in evidence a journal in Castro's hand with a note appended to his signature: "Rodger (sic) Charles Tichborne, Bart, some day, I hope."

Not only did the jury find the claimant guilty, they said they believed him to be Arthur Orton, formerly of Wapping, and protested that there was no evidence that the deceased Roger Tichborne had been "guilty of undue familiarity" with Katherine Doughty. The judge sentenced the claimant to two jail terms of seven years each to run consecutively. Released in 1884, the former butcher tried, but failed, to win back his supporters and died 14 years later in a cheap boarding house, still calling himself Sir Roger Tichborne.

Another long-running imposture was that of Stanley Weyman, born Weinberg, who assumed many roles in his career of distancing himself from his humble origins in Brooklyn. Money was only one of his objectives: he yearned to live on a grand scale and to hobnob with statesmen.

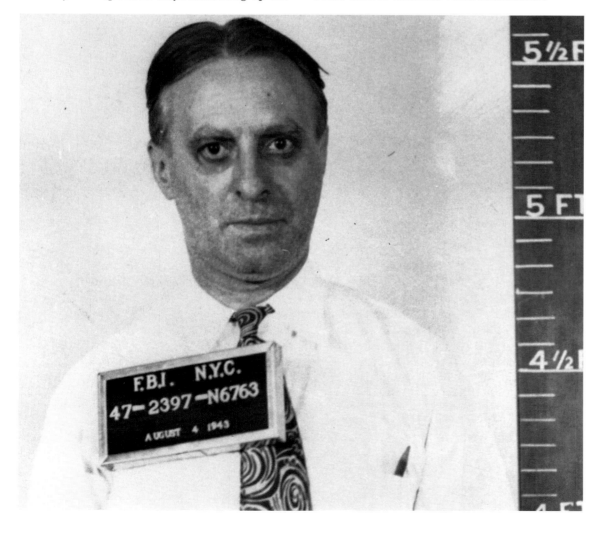

LEFT: Stanley Clifford Weyman, born Stephen Weinberg, one of the truly great impersonators. In his career he succeeded in conning the U.S. Navy into giving him a state visit to the battleship *Wyoming* as the Romanian consul-general; he attended a White House reception for Princess Fatima of Afghanistan as the State Department's chief of protocol; he claimed to have attended Rudolph Valentino as his physician; and became United Nations correspondent for the Erwin News Service.

RIGHT: Stanley Weyman most audacious con made the newspapers. Here, he (far right) poses with Princess Fatima of Afghanistan and her sons during the visit to the White House to meet with President Warren Harding in July 1921.

Weyman had all the attributes a confidence man needs, including quick wits, a plausible manner, and the ability to adapt to any situation. It was his penchant for impressive uniforms that often got him into trouble.

At the age of 21, he stole a camera while impersonating the U.S. consul-delegate to Morocco (in whose name he had run up several large restaurant bills) and was sent to reform school; he returned two years later for impersonating a naval officer. In 1915, at the age of 24, he represented himself to the U.S. Navy Department's New York office as the Romanian consul-general and requested a state visit to the battleship *Wyoming*.

Resplendent in a light-blue uniform trimmed in gold braid, he crossed New York Harbor in a launch to inspect a guard of honor and visit the officers' wardroom. There he invited everyone to dinner at the Hotel Astor. A New York detective saw the press release bearing the name of Stanley Weyman and had him arrested at the dinner table, to the consternation of the *Wyoming*'s officers, one of whom told reporters that "That little guy put on a hell of a show!"

Two years later, he was arrested while inspecting a regimental armory in Brooklyn dressed as an Army Air Corps officer. Since he wasn't making any money with these impersonations, he soon turned to a pseudo-medical career as consultant to a construction company working in Peru. His year-long stay was marked by extravagant parties at the company villa.

In 1921 Weyman reached the pinnacle of his career as an impostor by crashing the White House with Princess Fatima of Afghanistan. The princess was in New York on an unofficial visit when Lieutenant-Commander Weyman appeared at her suite in the Waldorf Astoria to invite her to Washington, where President Warren G. Harding wished to receive her. He explained that he was not only a naval officer, but the State Department's chief of protocol, and added that it was customary to give monetary gifts to junior officials who arranged such visits. Ten thousand dollars changed hands.

Weyman then telephoned the State Department in her name and obtained access to the president (security was looser in those days). The whole party traveled to Washington and posed for photographs with Harding before Weyman absconded with the money he had received for the hotel bill and alleged bribes to the media. It was some time before he was arrested again, this time for impersonating a hospital official.

When silent-film idol Rudolf Valentino

died, Weyman surfaced in Hollywood as the star's friend and physician. He was involved in the funeral arrangements and served for a time as the doctor of Pola Negri, who had played the vamp to Valentino's smoldering Latin lover. When that palled, he became a lawyer for a while, then a visiting lecturer to various universities. During World War II, he went into business and was also jailed for draft-dodging.

After the war, Weyman turned to journalism, at which he proved adept. He worked with several radio stations and became the United Nations correspondent for the Erwin News Service. At the U.N., the ambassador from Thailand offered him a job as press

RIGHT: Pola Negri (in the veil) leaves the funeral of screen idol Rudolph Valentino. Weyman helped with the star's funeral arrangements and became Negri's personal doctor for a time.

LEFT: The smoldering Latin looks that made Rudolph Valentino a Hollywood heart throb. Wealth, power and prestige, however, did not prevent him from being used in Weyman's con games.

BELOW: Ferdinand Waldo Demara's unprepossessing looks disguise the fact that he can lay claim to being one of the greatest impostors of the twentieth century. In his career he posed as a high-powered academic, a biology teacher and, most remarkably of all, naval surgeon Dr. Joseph Cyr who served in the Korean War.

officer to his delegation – a post that carried full diplomatic accreditation. However, the State Department dusted off its file on Stanley Weyman and the job fell through, along with his association with the Erwin News Service.

Weyman vanished into obscurity for the next nine years, to reappear, sadly, as the victim of an armed robber who held up the Yonkers, New York, motel where he was working as a night manager. In attempting to resist the robbery, he was shot and killed.

The puzzling career of Ferdinand Waldo Demara, "the Great Impostor," has defied explanation for many years. His nickname comes from the book of the same title written by Robert Crichton several years after Demara disappeared from public view in 1952. At the time, he was only 31 years old, but he had already lived a very full life – mostly as other people.

Demara was born into comfortable circumstances in Lawrence, Massachusetts, in 1921. But when he was 12 years old his father, a movie theater owner, went bankrupt and the family lost both security and

FAR RIGHT: Demara (left) is brought to account in Los Angeles during August 1964 for the relatively minor offense of stealing a station wagon. By this time, his days as the "Great Impostor" appeared over.

BELOW: True fame for the "Great Impostor." Here, Tony Curtis, playing Demara, enjoys a frugal meal in a monastery.

status. Apparently, young Fred, as he was called, could not adjust to the changed circumstances: he left home at 16 and joined a Cistercian monastery in Valley Falls, Rhode Island.

A year later, he moved on to a teaching order, the Brothers of Christian Charity, where he remained for three years before enlisting in the army. He promptly went AWOL and joined the navy a week later. After failing to qualify for Officer Candidate School, despite forged credentials from Iowa State College, he left his post at a hospital school in Norfolk, Virginia, and the navy with it. But he had acquired an interest in medicine that would alter his life and others'.

From Norfolk, Demara traveled to the Trappist monastery of Gethsemane near Louisville, Kentucky. There he presented himself as Robert L. French, a name he had gleaned from a college catalogue along with

an impressive background, including a Ph.D. in psychology from Stanford and a Sterling Research Fellowship from Yale. When life with the Trappists proved too quiet for him, he moved to a teaching order and studied scholastic philosophy at De Paul University, where he earned high marks.

However, his deceptions were catching up with him emotionally, as he admitted later: "In this little game I was playing, there always comes a time when you find yourself getting in too deep. You've made good friends who believe in you, and you don't want them to get hurt and disillusioned. You begin to worry about what they'll think if somebody exposes you as a phony."

Another pressing problem was his desertion from the military services. He was subject to arrest at any time, and the fear of this kept him on the run. For a time, Demara

ABOVE: Demara – Tony Curtis – assuming the identity of Dr. Joseph Cyr. In this guise Demara joined the Royal Canadian Navy and served on the destroyer *Cayuga*, performing complex surgery on wounded men based on information gleaned from medical textbooks. Remarkably, his patients recovered. Only when his exploits on behalf of the Korean War's wounded became common knowledge was he unmasked by the real Dr. Cyr.

considered ordination to the priesthood. But as he said later, ''I couldn't go ahead without telling those men the truth about myself. So I disappeared.''

A year later, he was teaching psychology at Gannon College in Erie, Pennsylvania. From there he migrated to Los Angeles, where he worked as a hospital orderly, and thence to Olympia, Washington, where he resumed his identity as Professor French to secure a position at St. Martin's College. He was well liked in Olympia, where he served as a deputy sheriff for the college campus, but the FBI caught up with him there and he was arrested for desertion of the navy.

Court-martialed, Demara was sentenced to 18 months in the U.S. Disciplinary Barracks at San Pedro, California. There he was an easy target for army investigators, who finally gave him a dishonorable discharge. The only advantage was that he would no longer have to dodge the military authorities.

After leaving prison, Demara resorted to his college-catalogue file and became Dr. Cecil B. Hamann, a college instructor in biology. This got him a position on the faculty of a parochial school in Alfred,

Maine, run by the Christian Brothers of Instruction. His old interest in medicine revived and he became friendly with a Dr. Joseph Cyr, who unwittingly provided him with a new identify as a doctor.

Taking leave of the Christian Brothers before they could ordain him, Demara joined the Royal Canadian Navy, then serving in the Korean War, as Dr. Cyr. He was given the rank of Lieutenant-Surgeon and posted to the destroyer *Cayuga* as a medical officer. Aboard the destroyer, he relied on his navy hospital training and his experience as an orderly to perform minor surgery and treat common ailments.

Before long, his surgical skills, acquired solely through poring over medical textbooks, were put to the test. He removed a bullet lodged near the heart of a Korean soldier, using the captain's cabin as an operating room. Then, amazingly, he performed a lung resection (removal) at an emergency aid station. Both patients recovered, but Demara was shocked by the conditions in which wounded South Koreans were convalescing and made efforts to secure better care for them.

As a result, the public relations officer aboard the *Cayuga* released a story to the press about the heroic Dr. Cyr, which was read by the real Dr. Cyr, who promptly denounced Demara as an impostor. The Royal Canadian Navy returned him to the United States, where a board of surgeons dismissed him for giving fraudulent medical treatment.

Demara's last known imposture was as a Connecticut teacher named Martin Godgart. In this guise, he got a teaching position in North Haven, Maine, where he was well liked and active in the community as a scout leader. An old picture of him in *Life* magazine brought an end to his career there, and his parting words to *Life*, which printed his story in 1952, were "I don't know what I'm going to do next." The world is still waiting to find out.

One of the saddest stories in the annals of imposture is that of Anna Anderson, claimant to the role of Grand Duchess Anastasia, the 16-year-old daughter of the last Romanov czar of Russia. She was massacred with her whole family at Ekaterinburg (now Sverdlovsk) in 1918, but, as with the Lost Dauphin, rumors of her survival and escape circulated for many years.

In 1920 a German speaking woman who called herself Anna Anderson was prevented from committing suicide in Berlin, where she tried to jump into a canal. The police committed her, at her own request, to the mental institution at Daldorf, where she spent two years, refusing to identify herself. Finally, she stated that she was Anastasia, the only surviving child of Czar Nicholas II and heir to the Romanov estates and fortune. She told a complex tale of rescue from

LEFT: Is this the face of the true Grand Duchess Anastasia or just a con artist? Anna Anderson, a German-speaking woman revealed herself to be Anastasia, claiming that she had survived the Bolshevik firing squad that had killed the rest of her family in 1918. Relatives of the Romanov family agreed that she bore a strong resemblance to Anastasia and her body was covered in scars inflicted by bullets and bayonets. Although she maintained her claim until her death, she was never accepted as the missing princess.

BELOW: Anna Anderson pictured in old age. There is little doubt that she believed in the justness of her claim to be the only surviving member of the Romanovs, but she was never able to convince those who might have upheld her claim.

the massacre by an anti-Bolshevik soldier whom she later married and who was killed by the Bolsheviks.

Some members of the Romanov family, and their employees, came to the hospital at a nurse's request and confirmed that Anna bore a strong physical resemblance to Anastasia. Multiple bullet and bayonet scars on her body seemed to prove her story, and she was released from the hospital in 1922. However, disbelievers accused her of being a Polish orphan named Franziska Schanzkowski who had disappeared from a Berlin boarding house at the time Anna tried to commit suicide. The German House of Hesse, related to the Czarina Alexandra, repudiated her story possibly because they stood to acquire the Romanov inheritance. Nevertheless, ''Anastasia'' continued to assert her claims for another 65 years. There is no doubt that she believed to the end of her life that she was the last of the imperial Romanovs of Russia – the last princess of the Russian Empire.

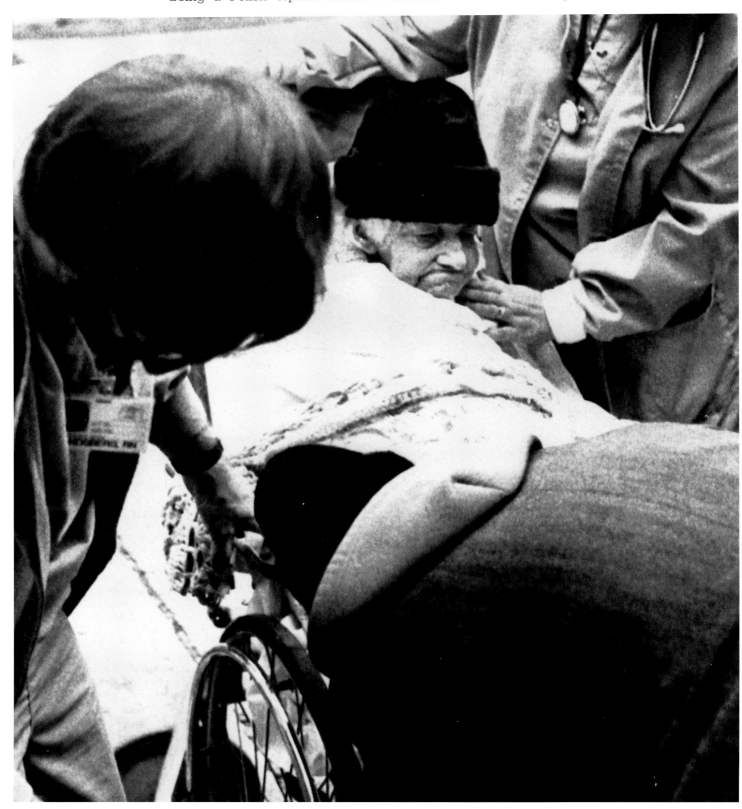

Index

Page numbers in *italics* refer to illustrations.

Acknowledgments

The publisher would like to thank Ron
Callow of D-23 for designing this book, Rita
Longabucco and Suzanne O'Farrell for the
picture research, and Ron Watson for
compiling the index. The following
provided illustrative material:

Agencia ANSA, Rome, page: 81.
Professor Quentin Bell, page: 33
(bottom).
The Bettmann Archive, pages: 1, 2-3 (all),
13 (both), 14 (all three), 16, 25 (both), 28, 36,
38, 39 (both), 40 (both), 41, 42, 43 (top), 44,
45, 46, 47, 53, 54, 55 (all three), 56 (top), 57
(bottom), 59 (both), 61 (bottom), 62 (both),
78, 79, 96, 98, 99, 102 (right), 103 (both),
104, 106, 107, 108, 109.
**The Bettmann Archive/Hulton Picture
Library**, page: 33 (top).
Bonhams, London, page: 95 (Bridgeman
Art Library).
The British Library, London, pages: 32,
50, 51 (both), 110, 111, 112, 116.
The British Museum, London, pages: 21
(bottom), 22, 23, 80, 86-87.
Brompton Books Limited, pages: 14
(bottom), 69, 122, 124.
Chicago Historical Society, page: 67.
© **Collection Viollet, Paris**, pages: 114,
115.
Diário de Noticias, Portugal, pages: 29,
30, 31.
Giraudon, page: 60 (Bridgeman Art
Library).
**Hulton-Deutsch Collection Limited,
London**, pages: 90, 125.
The Imperial War Museum, London,
pages: 18, 34, 35 (both).
The Mansell Collection, page: 57 (top).
**Museum Boymans van Beuningen,
Rotterdam, Holland**, page: 91.
The National Galleries of Scotland,
page: 27 (top).
The National Gallery, London, page: 83
**The National Maritime Museum,
London**, page: 101.
The National Portrait Gallery, London,
pages 20, 24, 56 (bottom).
Richard Natkiel, page: 21 (top).
The Natural History Museum, London,
pages: 4-5.
Reuters/Bettmann Newsphotos, pages:
17, 75 (both), 88-89.
Springer/Bettmann Film Archives,
page: 6.
The Tate Gallery, London, pages: 52-53.
UPI/Bettmann Newsphotos, pages: 8, 9,
10-11, 26, 27 (bottom), 44 (bottom), 63, 64,
65, 68-69, 70 (both), 71, 72, 73, 74 (both), 84
(both), 85, 92, 93, 94, 102 (left), 105, 106, 117,
118-119, 120, 121 (both), 123, 126.
U.S. Library of Congress, pages: 66, 101.
U.S. National Archives, pages: 12, 82.